Portage Public Library

$19.95

**Cultural and Geographical Exploration**

# The Russian People in 1914
**CHRONICLES FROM *NATIONAL GEOGRAPHIC***

## Cultural and Geographical Exploration

Ancient Civilizations of the Aztecs and Maya

The Ancient Incas

Australia: The Unique Continent

Building the Panama Canal

Grand Canyon Experiences

Hawaii and the Islands of the Pacific:
A Visit to the South Seas

Indian Tribes of the Americas

Jerusalem and the Holy Land

Lighthouses: Beacons of the Sea

Mysteries of the Sahara

Race for the South Pole—The Antarctic Challenge

Rediscovering Ancient Egypt

Robert E. Peary and the Rush to the North Pole

The Russian People in 1914

Touring America Seventy-Five Years Ago

Touring China Eighty Years Ago

**Cultural and Geographical Exploration**

# The Russian People in 1914

### CHRONICLES FROM *NATIONAL GEOGRAPHIC*

Arthur M. Schlesinger, jr.
*Senior Consulting Editor*

Fred L. Israel
*General Editor*

CHELSEA HOUSE PUBLISHERS

*Philadelphia*

**CHELSEA HOUSE PUBLISHERS**

*Editor in Chief* Stephen Reginald
*Managing Editor* James D. Gallagher
*Production Manager* Pamela Loos
*Art Director* Sara Davis
*Director of Photography* Judy L. Hasday
*Senior Production Editor* LeeAnne Gelletly

© 2000 by Chelsea House Publishers, a division of Main Line Book Co. All rights reserved. Printed and bound in the United States of America.

The Chelsea House World Wide Web site address is
http://www.chelseahouse.com

First Printing

1 3 5 7 9 8 6 4 2

Library of Congress Cataloging-in-Publication Data

The Russian people in 1914 / [edited and with an introduction by] Fred L. Israel.
    p. cm. — (Cultural and geographical exploration)
    Includes bibliographical references and index.
    ISBN 0-7910-5446-2 (hardcover)
    1. Russia—Social life and customs—1533-1917 Juvenile literature.
    I. Israel, Fred L.  II. Series.
DK262.R875  1999
947.08'3—dc21                    99-20056                              CIP

---

This work is neither endorsed by, nor sponsored by, nor affiliated with the National Geographic Society or any of its publications.

# CONTENTS

"The Greatest Educational Journal"
    *by Fred L. Israel* ............................................vi
The Russian People in 1914
    *by Fred L. Israel* ............................................ix

Young Russia: The Land of Unlimited
    Possibilities..................................................1

    Further Reading....................................105
    Index......................................................107
    Contributors.........................................111

# "THE GREATEST EDUCATIONAL JOURNAL"

When the first *National Geographic* magazine appeared in October 1888, the United States totaled 38 states. Grover Cleveland was President. The nation's population hovered around 60 million. Great Britain's Queen Victoria also ruled as the Empress of India. William II became Kaiser of Germany that year. Czar Alexander III ruled Russia, and the Turkish Empire stretched from the Balkans to the tip of Arabia. To Westerners, the Far East was still a remote and mysterious land. Throughout the world, riding the back of an animal was the principal means of transportation. Unexplored and unmarked places dotted the global map.

On January 13, 1888, thirty-three men—scientists, cartographers, inventors, scholars, and explorers—met in Washington, D.C. They had accepted an invitation from Gardiner Greene Hubbard (1822–1897), the first president of the Bell Telephone Company and a leader in the education of the deaf, to form the National Geographic Society "to increase and diffuse geographic knowledge." One of the assembled group noted that they were the "first explorers of the Grand Canyon and the Yellowstone, those who had carried the American flag farthest north, who had measured the altitude of our famous mountains, traced the windings of our coasts and rivers, determined the distribution of flora and fauna, enlightened us in the customs of the aborigines, and marked out the path of storm and flood." Nine months later, the first issue of *National Geographic* magazine was sent out to 165 charter members. Today, more than a century later, membership has grown to an astounding 11 million in more than 170 nations. Several times that number regularly read the monthly issues of the *National Geographic* magazine.

The first years were difficult ones for the new magazine. The earliest volumes seem dreadfully scientific and quite dull. The articles in Volume I, No. 1 set the tone—W. M. Davis, "Geographic Methods in Geologic Investigation," followed by W. J. McGee, "The Classification of Geographic Forms by Genesis." Issues came out erratically—three in 1889, five in 1890, four in 1891; and two in 1895. In January 1896 "an illustrated monthly" was added to the title. The November issue that year contained a photograph of a half-naked Zulu bride and bridegroom in their wedding finery staring full face into the camera. But, a reader must have wondered what to make of the accompanying text: "These people . . . possess some excellent traits, but are horribly cruel when once they have smelled blood." In hopes of expanding circulation, the Board of Managers offered newsstand copies at $.25 each and began to accept advertising. But the magazine essentially remained unchanged. Circulation rose only slightly.

In January 1898, shortly after Gardiner Greene Hubbard's death, his son-in-law Alexander Graham Bell (1847–1922) agreed to succeed him as the second president of the National Geographic Society. Bell invented the telephone in 1876 and, while pursuing his lifelong goal of improving the lot of the deaf, had turned his amazingly versatile mind to contemplating such varied problems as human flight, air conditioning, and popularizing geography. The society then had about 1,100 members—the magazine was on the edge of bankruptcy. Bell did not want the job. He wrote in his diary, though, that he accepted leadership of the society "in order to save it." "Geography is a fascinating subject and it can be made interesting," he told the board of directors. Bell abandoned the unsuccessful attempt to increase circulation through newsstand sales. "Our journal," he wrote, "should go to members, people who believe in our work and want to help." He understood that the lure for prospective members should be an association with a society that made it possible for the average person to share with kings and scientists the excitement of sending an expedition to a strange land or an explorer to an inaccessible region. This idea, more than any other, has been responsible for the growth of the National Geographic Society and for the popularity of the magazine. "I can well remember," recalled Bell in 1912, "how the idea was laughed at that we should ever reach a membership of ten thousand." That year it had soared to 107,000!

Bell attributed this phenomenal growth, though, to one man who had transformed the *National Geographic* magazine into "the greatest educational journal in the world"—Gilbert H. Grosvenor (1875–1966). Bell had hired Grosvenor, then 24, in 1899 as the National Geographic Society's first full-time employee, "to put some life into the magazine." He personally escorted the new editor, who would become his son-in-law, to the society's headquarters—a small rented room shared with the American Forestry Association on the fifth floor of a building near the U.S. Treasury in downtown Washington. Grosvenor remembered the headquarters "littered with old magazines, newspapers, and a few record books and six enormous boxes crammed with *Geographics* returned by the newsstands." "No desk!" exclaimed Bell. "I'll send you mine." That afternoon, delivery men brought Grosvenor a large walnut rolltop and the new editor began to implement Bell's instructions—to transform the magazine from one of cold geographic fact "expressed in hieroglyphic terms which the layman could not understand into a vehicle for carrying the living, breathing, human-interest truth about this great world of ours to the people." And what did Bell consider appropriate "geographic subjects"? He replied: "The world and all that is in it is our theme."

Grosvenor shared Bell's vision of a great society and magazine that would disseminate geographic knowledge. "I thought of geography in terms of its Greek root: *geographia*—a description of the world," he later wrote. "It thus becomes the most catholic of subjects, universal in appeal, and embracing nations, people, plants, birds, fish. We would never lack interesting subjects." To attract readers, Grosvenor had to change the public attitude toward geography, which he knew was regarded as "one of the dullest of all subjects, something to inflict upon schoolboys and avoid in later life." He wondered why certain books that relied heavily on geographic description remained popular—Charles Darwin's *Voyage of the Beagle*, Richard Dana Jr.'s *Two Years Before the Mast*, and even Herodotus's *History*. Why did readers for generations—and with Herodotus's travels, for 20 centuries—return to these books? What did these volumes, which used so many geographic descriptions, have in common? What was the secret? According to Grosvenor, the answer was that "each was an accurate, eyewitness, firsthand account. Each contained simple straightforward writing—writing that sought to make pictures in the reader's mind."

# The Russian People in 1914

Gilbert Grosvenor was editor of the *National Geographic* magazine for 55 years, from 1899 until 1954. Each of the 660 issues under his direction had been a highly readable geography textbook. He took Bell's vision and made it a reality. Acclaimed as "Mr. Geography," he discovered the earth anew for himself and for millions around the globe. He charted the dynamic course that the National Geographic Society and its magazine followed for more than half a century. In so doing, he forged an instrument for world education and understanding unique in this or any age. Under his direction, the *National Geographic* magazine grew in circulation from a few hundred copies—he recalled carrying them to the post office on his back—to more than five million at the time of his retirement as editor, enough for a stack 25 miles high.

This Chelsea House series celebrates Grosvenor's first 25 years as editor of the *National Geographic*. "The mind must see before it can believe," said Grosvenor. From the earliest days, he filled the magazine with photographs and established another Geographic principle—to portray people in their natural attire or lack of it. Within his own editorial committee, young Grosvenor encountered the prejudice that photographs had to be "scientific." Too often, this meant dullness. To Grosvenor, every picture and sentence had to be interesting to the layperson. "How could you educate and inform if you lost your audience by boring your readers?" Grosvenor would ask his staff. He persisted and succeeded in making the *National Geographic* magazine reflect this fascinating world.

To the young-in-heart of every age there is magic in the name *National Geographic*. The very words conjure up enchanting images of faraway places, explorers and scientists, sparkling seas and dazzling mountain peaks, strange plants, animals, people, and customs. The small society founded in 1888 "for the increase and diffusion of geographic knowledge" grew, under the guidance of one man, to become a great force for knowledge and understanding. This achievement lies in the genius of Gilbert H. Grosvenor, the architect and master builder of the National Geographic Society and its magazine.

Fred L. Israel
*The City College of the City University of New York*

# THE RUSSIAN PEOPLE IN 1914

## Fred L. Israel

At the beginning of the 20th century, the Russian Empire stretched from Poland in the west to the Pacific Ocean in the east, extending into the Arctic north and reaching the Black Sea and the borders of Turkey and Afghanistan in the south. The empire was twice as large as Europe—occupying three-fifths of that continent and nearly two-fifths of Asia. The Russian Empire was so large, it was just 10 longitudinal degrees short of reaching halfway around the earth and covered one-sixth of the globe's total land area. The hub of the empire, European Russia, had a population of about 92 million in 1897, with the nation's total population at 129.4 million in that year's official census.

The Russian czars presented to the world a brilliant image of monarchical power and opulence. The rituals of homage to the dynasty and the glorification of its history were meant to inspire reverence and popular support for the principle of autocracy. Russia stood as a great European power.

However, its society was far less developed than that of Great Britain, France, or Germany, thanks to persistent neglect of education by the nation's rulers. In 1897, less than a tenth of 1 percent of the population of the Russian Empire had attended or were attending a university or institute of higher education, and nearly all of these were children of nobles or of government officials. Fewer than 1 percent had been to any sort of secondary school; 40 percent of this group were the children of nobles and officials. In 1904, only 27 percent of school-age children attended a primary school. Illiteracy was rampant, with less than 40 percent of the population able to read or write.

A widely reprinted 1901 cartoon depicted six layers of Russian society. In the illustration, the top five layers—the czar, his ministers, the clergy, the army, the middle class—are all being held up by the bottom layer, the peasants. Poverty-stricken peasants made up five-sixths of the population. Until the mid-19th century, this large group of people had been serfs—the lowest members of a feudal system that had bound them to the land they worked and subjected them to the arbitrary will of the landowner. By the 1850s, serfdom seemed not only unjust but intolerable and was a major obstacle to economic development. In 1861 Czar Alexander II freed the Russian serfs.

Unfortunately, the emancipation process was slow and complex. The new peasant class, with government loans, had to "redeem" their land allotment from the landlords and make "redemption payments" to the government for the next 49 years. In the revolutionary year of 1905, the government terminated these payments, but the peasants remained poor and desperate for land of their own.

The Russian Empire was multilingual and multireligious. But only half the population could be considered Russian by language and orthodox by religion. The monarchy attached great importance to the Russian Orthodox Church by bestowing upon it the status of the nation's religion and granting it enormous privilege; but all Christians, regardless of denomination, enjoyed a better status than did the Muslims and Jews. The Russian Orthodox Church taught that only its adherents were true Russians. A Jew, for example, no matter how patriotic and assimilated into the national culture, remained an outsider.

More than 100 different nationalities lived under the autocratic rule of the czar. Russians lived almost everywhere in the vast empire. Land-hungry peasants even had been encouraged to settle in Siberia and in czarist possessions in central Asia. To further complicate matters, almost all peasants identified more with their villages than with any imperial nationalistic ideas.

Industrial growth at the beginning of the 20th century had created an urban working class that was unskilled, meagerly paid, and poorly housed. Uprooted from rural villages, peasants flocked to the new industrial centers hoping for a better life. But the surplus of laborers made working conditions deplorable. In 1897, the government decreed a maximum working day of $11^1/_2$ hours for all workers, both male and female, and 10 hours for those engaged in night work. Trade unions were outlawed. A new elite business class developed. But government policies, rather than a free market, dominated. Hence, Russian businessmen sided with the autocracy.

In the spring of 1914, Gilbert H. Grosvenor, the editor of the *National Geographic*, visited Russia. He wrote the following article and took the photographs. Grosvenor referred to Russia as a "youth among the nations," just beginning to grow. The purpose of his essay was to show the vitality of the Russian people, "more than half of whom lived in bondage in the lifetime of thousands of our readers." He was optimistic that new farming techniques, as well as the introduction of modern conveniences—such as electricity, the telephone, and the railroad—into remote areas would end poverty and illiteracy and assist in transforming the Russian Empire into a land of unlimited possibilities.

Grosvenor's article is perceptive; however, it is also an account of a great nation just prior to the cataclysmic world war that would plunge Russia into a convulsive revolution three years later—a revolution whose reverberations would dramatically affect the world during the 20th century. Instead of Grosvenor's hope for Russia—peace and progress—chaos and confusion would dominate Russia in the decades to come.

# YOUNG RUSSIA
## The Land of Unlimited Possibilities

By Gilbert H. Grosvenor

RUSSIA is not a State; it is a world. Thus wrote a famous publicist of the land of the Tsar as he contemplated the diversity of origin of its peoples, its wide range of climate, its great variety of resources, and the dissimilarity of aspirations of the human elements of which the empire is composed.

In the blood of its people is written the impress of the Orient and of the Occident; of the tropic south and the frigid north; of Confucianism, Mohammedanism, and Christianity. Its range of climate gives the Palm Beach touch to its Crimea and the breath of the north to its White Sea region. Its variety of resources makes it second only to the United States as the greatest food-producing country in the world; places it at the forefront among the nations as to mineral wealth, and gives it a greater timber supply than any other country. Its history borrows from Mongol-land, Lapland, Finland; from the Black Sea, the Baltic Sea, and the Okhotsk Sea. And its peoples have aspirations varying as widely as those of the Poles and the Mongols, as those of the Confucians and the Jews, as those of the Lapps and the Tatars.

In area Russia is the greatest compact empire on the face of the earth. It is larger than all of North America, larger than the combined area of the United States and Alaska, Canada, Mexico and Central America, Cuba, Porto Rico, Haiti, and the other islands of the Caribbean thrown in, and has a total area of 8,505,000 square miles as compared with South America's 6,851,000. The British Empire may be larger, but Britain must girdle the globe to find her people, and traverse the seven seas and the six continents to locate her possessions. Russia is more than twice as big as Europe, and occupies three-fifths of the area of that continent; it is half as big as Asia, and occupies nearly two-fifths of its area. Within its boundaries are embraced two-fifths of all territory of Europe and Asia combined. The Empire holds nearly one and a half times as much land in Asia as China has; its Asiatic possessions are three times as great as those of Great Britain, and they are forty times as great as those of Japan, even since the new Asiatic balance that followed the Russo-Japanese War was struck.

### A TRIAL STATUE IN FRONT OF THE UNIVERSITY: NIZHNI-NOVGOROD

Before erecting a statue in Russia it is customary to submit the design to the vote of the people. On the left of this picture is shown one of these trial statues—an outline in wood and chalk of a memorial proposed to the prince, Pojarski, and the butcher, Minin, who aroused the Russians in 1613 and drove the Poles out of Russia. People are urged to send in criticisms to the municipal authorities, with a frank statement whether the design is liked or not. If the majority do not approve the design, it is withdrawn and another substituted for criticism until a satisfactory one is obtained. The custom has resulted in Russia having probably the best memorial groups and statues of any country.

### A CART OF BELLS ON THE WAY TO MARKET: NIZHNI-NOVGOROD

Russia is the land of bells; the biggest bells in the world are those at Moscow (see pages 15–18).

MEDALS OF SERVICE

This decorated individual is not a high officer or the hero of many battlefields, but the messenger at police headquarters in Petrograd. Permission to take photographs must be obtained from the police in every city or town, and this necessitates a personal visit to headquarters. This man occupies the lowest position on the police staff and was delighted to pose for his picture. The medals denote length of service, presence at an anniversary of the Tsar, etc., and are greatly prized.

## RICH IN ALL RESPECTS BUT ONE

Indeed, Russia lacks but ten degrees of reaching half way around the earth, and possesses one-sixth of the landed area of the globe. It is divided into more than a hundred provinces—corresponding generally to our States—the largest of which is as much bigger than our imperial State of Texas as the Lone Star State is larger than Virginia.

But with all its geographic greatness Russia is about as poor in natural outlets to the world as the smallest of the countries of the earth. Holland could be hidden in the vast reaches of the Russian plain, almost as a needle in a haystack, and yet Amsterdam alone does more international business than all the seaports of Russia together. Not one free outlet to the open sea does European Russia possess except on the ice-bound shores of the Arctic Ocean. Petrograd and Riga find their waterways to the sea only through the narrow straits that divide Germany and Sweden and Denmark and Norway. On the Black Sea is Odessa, with its immense harbor works, but the path from the Black Sea to the Mediterranean leads through the narrow channels of the Bosphorus and Dardanelles, held by alien hands. Asiatic Russia possesses Vladivostock as an outlet to the Pacific, but that is 2,000 miles farther from Petrograd than New York is distant from San Francisco, and a home port nearly 6,000 miles away is almost as distant in influence as though it were foreign.

## THE MOST PROLIFIC PEOPLE ON EARTH

If Russia is an empire in the extent of its dominions, it is none the less so in the number of its people. Within its boundaries and under its flag live enough people to populate the United Kingdom, the German Empire, and the French Republic, with enough left over to repopulate half of the dual monarchy of Austria-Hungary.

Nor has Russia reached the limits of its human resources if it shall emerge from the war with the integrity of its territory maintained. Its 172,000,000 people are the most fecund on earth. During the 40 years from 1872 to 1912 European Russia, notwithstanding her excessive death rate, doubled her population and the larger ratio of that growth was toward the end rather than toward the beginning of that period. Assuming that the same ratio will keep up, at the end of the present century Russia will have over six hundred million people—enough to offset the present population of all the continents except Asia.

## RUSSIA, A YOUNG NATION COMPARED TO ENGLAND

From such a record of size, of bigness in everything, we should expect Russia to be an old nation, like Great Britain, with perhaps a thousand years of unhindered growth behind her. But, as a matter of fact, Russia is a youth among the nations compared to England, a stripling whose full stature and breadth are still a subject of conjecture and speculation.

Russia is young because she never had a chance to grow until recent years. Her geographical shape or condition was such that for centuries her people were constantly being enslaved or despoiled by stronger neighbors.

European Russia is an enormous plain 2,000 miles long and about a thousand miles wide. In it there are no mountains and no hills more than a few hundred feet high. It is so flat that the rivers are sluggish and tortuous, and seem uncertain in which direction to flow. For instance, its greatest river, the Volga, 2,400 miles long, has an average drop of only 4 inches to the mile. This plain served as a highway for the successive barbaric hordes on their way from Asia to western Europe.

The Russian Slavs, whose origin we will not discuss in this brief article, were among the last to come, settling in the western portion of the Russian plain. On all sides of them were enemies—Finns, Swedes, Lithuanians, Poles, and Tatars. The plain offered a splendid arena for fighting, and as there were no geographical

### A TRAFFIC POLICEMAN: PETROGRAD

The official in Russia who has not at least six medals to display is unhappy indeed; but the medals are not worn in a spirit of vanity. Their possession gives self–confidence and inspires devotion, not arrogance or conceit. The Russian likes to feel that his zeal, faithfulness, and ability are recognized by his superiors, and wears his decorations constantly, so that all may see them. Nor does the fact that medals are almost as common as buttons give them any less distinction or value. This policeman was originally a moujik, for the peasants, with training and experience, make splendid policemen and soldiers. Nowhere in Europe is there a finer body of men than the policemen in Petrograd, Moscow, Nizhni-Novgorod, and the other big cities of Russia, all of them originally peasants.

### PASSING A SHRINE IN MOSCOW

Moscow is a city of shrines and churches. In every square and on every street corner there is some holy picture before which the devout uncover and make the sign of the Russian cross. This picture shows on the right one of these street shrines—an icon before which a candle is burning and a tankard of holy water. The passer-by may take a sip of the holy water from the common cup. The cab driver has uncovered and is making the sign of the cross as he rattles by.

fences to keep them out, these enemies were incessantly attacking the Russians, devastating their fields and burning their wooden cities, making it necessary for the unfortunate inhabitants continually to rebuild. As a result, there is nothing old in Russia—no ancient fortresses like the feudal castles of the Rhine and the Danube, no walled cities like Wisby, in Gotland, or some of the noted towns of Germany.

If the Russians had not been one of the most prolific races the world has ever known, they would have been obliterated in those bit-

### THE HORIZON OF MOSCOW IS MARKED BY
### COUNTLESS GILDED SPIRES AND STARRY DOMES

The Russians call Moscow "Holy Mother Moscow," because it is the center around which grew the Russian Empire and Russian church. There are 500 churches and cathedrals in Moscow and many hundreds of shrines; (1) indicates Bell Tower, see p. 8, and (2) St. Basils, see p. 75.

ter years. Only a race of extraordinary vitality, of extraordinary tenacity could have survived what they suffered.

## MOSCOW IS THE MOTHER OF RUSSIA

European Russia, as we know it, gradually grew from Moscow as a center—Mother Moscow, the Russians call her. An old Slavic prince was attracted by a small hill, probably not over 100 feet high, on the Moshva River, in the heart of this great plain. It seemed to him to be the best natural fortress within many miles. So on this little eminence, which would not have been noticed as having military value in any other country of Europe, he built a fort, surrounded with high wooden walls and deep moats. It became known as the Kremlin, and within the fortress soon gathered merchants and traders who brought considerable population and wealth.

But it could not escape the torch and greedy clutch of the Tatar. In 1237 the Golden Horde laid waste the country, burned Moscow to the last house, and slew the reigning prince The city was rebuilt, then again burned to the ground, in 1380, by another Tatar mob, though meanwhile the princes of Moscow had been paying heavy tribute to the Tatar Khan. "The Tatars slew without mercy; 24,000 perished. They broke into the churches and treasuries, pillaged everywhere, and burned a mass of books, papers, and whatever they could not otherwise destroy; not a house was left standing save the few built of stone."

But the princes of Moscow were shrewd and patient, their people the most enduring and prolific in history. Again they rebuilt the city, and Moscow soon became more prosperous than ever, with many fine churches and monasteries.

After Constantinople had fallen before the Turkish sword and the Byzantine Empire disappeared, the niece and heiress of the last Constantine, Sophia, married the Prince of Moscow, Ivan III. She brought to the Russian royal house the double-headed eagle, which for 1,000 years had been the emblem of the Byzantine Empire,

### VIEW OF THE KREMLIN, MOSCOW, SHOWING THE HIGH
### WALL AND LOFTY WATCH-TOWERS WHICH INCLOSE IT

The Kremlin is the keystone of Russian history. The men who lived and ruled in it were those who, out of a collection of petty and weak princedoms, created the mighty Russian Empire. Originally a fort, it is now museum, mausoleum, and treasure house of things precious in Russian life and Russian religion. In no other equal area in the world is there crowded such an array of historic cathedrals and monasteries, sacred relics, trophies of war, sacerdotal robes, tombs of human saints and human devils, gold and silver vessels, precious stones, pearls, and jewels to the value of millions of dollars, etc.

The principal buildings, reading from the left, are: (I) Treasury and Museum; (2) Grand Palace; (3) Cathedral of Annunciation, where the Tsars are baptized and married; (4) Cathedral of Archangels, where all the Tsars were buried until Peter the Great; (5) Cathedral of Our Saviour behind the Golden Gate (see page 20); (6) Cathedral of Assumption, where all Tsars are crowned (see page 14); (7) The Bell Tower (see page 15); (8) Monastery of Miracles (see page 19).

but, more important than all in Russian eyes, she made Moscow the lawful heir to Constantinople and the head of the Greek Orthodox Church.

Sophia found the Tatar yoke unbearable, and kept asking her husband, "How long am I to be the slave of the Tatars?" Her husband had been most successful in overcoming neighboring princes and adding their domains to his principality, and finally, in 1478, when the customary messengers came from the Tatar Khan demanding the usual tribute, Ivan threw the edict on the ground, stamped and spat on it, and killed all the ambassadors save one, whom he sent back to his master. The enraged Tatars sought revenge, but their efforts availed naught against Ivan's armies.

## THE BATTLEMENTS OF THE KREMLIN: MOSCOW

In early days the walls of the fortress were built of oak, but the wooden walls yielded so often to fire that the princes of Moscow finally attempted to construct them of stone and brick. Though this period was three centuries after the English, French, and Germans had built lasting memorials in stone—Ely Cathedral, Notre Dame, Strasburg Cathedral, and many others—the Muscovites were still so ignorant of masonry construction that the walls they built soon fell to pieces. Ivan III, the same who married the heiress to Constantinople (see page 7), thereupon imported Italian architects and Italian masons, who erected the present imposing battlements and taught the people how to manufacture good brick and mortar.

## THE RESULTS OF TATAR RULE

Moscow, after nearly 300 years of subjection to the Tatars, was freed. But the hatred of Mohammedan rule had been bred in the bone of every Slav for ten generations—a hatred that has remained in the race to this day, and has prompted Russia always to help the oppressed in any fight to throw off the Mohammedan yoke. For this reason they were willing to sacrifice 379,000 lives in their wars against the Turk; to help Greece to freedom in 1828, and again Servia, Rumania, and Bulgaria in 1878, whereas no other European nation ever expended anything but words in behalf of the subject Christian; for this reason, Russia alone of the great Christian powers (England, France, and Germany) has not once been the ally of the Turk.

But the influence of the Tatar upon the blood of the Russian people has been much exaggerated. The expression, "Scratch a Russian and you find a Tatar underneath," is commonly attributed to Napoleon. If Napoleon did originate this remarkable statement, he partly revenged himself for his defeat, for the quotation is widely but wrongly accepted as a true description of the Russian. As a matter of fact, the Tatars did not settle among the Slavs. They were content to rule from afar, with periodic visitations to ravage and plunder, in order that there might be no delay in the remittance of tribute. But their contribution to the racial stock of Russia was comparatively little.

## IVAN THE TERRIBLE

Some years after the Ivan who married the heiress to Constantinople came another Ivan, called the Terrible, who assumed the title of Tsar, crushed the nobles, conquered Siberia, and extended his dominion to the Pacific. "All histories are spotless in comparison with that of Moscow under him—a creature of unparalleled ferocity and inconceivable wickedness. . . . He went to the torture-rooms with joy, and came away from its fiendish practices invigorated, refreshed, and gay."

This was the age of Shakespeare and Bacon in England.

Ivan slew his oldest son with his own hand in a fit of rage. His greatest crime was the sacking and destruction of the ancient city of Novgorod, whose infidelity he suspected. "The Tsar and his son went to an enclosure specially reserved for the torture of their victims, and with their lances prodded those who were not quickly enough dragged to the place of torment. Chroniclers say that from 500 to 1,000 were slain in cold blood before him each day of his stay. Some were burned, some racked to death, others drowned in the Volkhof, run in on sledges or thrown in from the bridge—soldiers in boats spearing those who swam. Infants were impaled before the eyes of their mothers, husbands butchered along with their wives. Novgorod, at that time larger and of greater commercial importance than Moscow, was so injured that she never since acquired the rank of even a third-rate town."

But in spite of his cruelty and superstition, Ivan was in many respects a successful ruler, reducing the Tatar kingdom and extending the Russian dominions to the Pacific by the help of a freebooter, Yermak, who swept the Siberian steppes as clean of Russian foes as Drake at the same time was clearing the seas for England. A hundred years before Peter the Great, Ivan "opened the Russian window to the West"—brought in the printing press and welcomed English sailors to his court. His ambassador, Nepeïa, in London, at the festival of the Garter, sat beside the Queen. "Never," the

### THE BEAUTIFUL REDEEMER GATE TO THE KREMLIN: MOSCOW

Every man when passing under this gate must uncover. In the old days all the religious processions left and entered the Kremlin by this gate, the metropolitan, or head of the church, heading the procession mounted on a donkey, which was led by the Tsar, bareheaded. When the Russians rose against the rule of the Poles, according to tradition, they forced their way into the Kremlin through this gate (1613), the metropolitan leading the way and carrying an icon of our Saviour behind him. Later this icon was mounted over the gate (see next page), and the Tsar, Alexis, ordered that any man who failed to uncover as he passed through should be compelled to prostrate himself 52 times.

**A NEAR VIEW OF THE HOLY OR REDEEMER GATE: MOSCOW**

Note that all the men have removed their hats. A burning candle is always kept in the lantern before the picture—the icon of Our Saviour (see page 11).

INSIDE THE HOLY GATE: MOSCOW

The women are bringing their babies to be blessed in the cathedrals and to obtain merit by kissing the relics, bones, etc.

Russian historian Karamzin naively says, "had the Russian name been honored to such a degree."

But after him came the whirlwind—years of greater misery and shame to the Russians than any they had yet experienced: a weak-minded ruler, interminable civil wars, a royal decree forbidding the peasants to leave the lands, thus reducing them to serfs or slaves; an impostor who actually seized and held the throne for one year,

## THE CATHEDRAL OF THE ASSUMPTION, WHERE
## THE TSARS ARE CROWNED, IN THE KREMLIN: MOSCOW

This magnificent structure was built near the end of the 16th century, to replace the old wooden church which had been repeatedly destroyed by fire. In it are many old icons and precious relics, among them "one of the nails with which our Lord was fastened to the cross, a fragment of His robe, and a fragment of the Virgin's robe; the hand of St. Andrew, the head of St. Gregory, the theologian, and that of St. John Crysostom."

    The icon of the Holy Virgin of Vladimir is pointed out as having been painted by St. Luke. It is adorned with jewels valued at half a million dollars, the splendid emerald alone being worth $50,000. Other treasures include a Bible presented by the mother of Peter the Great, which is so large that the services of two men are required to carry it. It also is studded with emeralds and precious stones. When Napoleon's army was in Moscow a cavalry regiment was stabled in the cathedral. The troops took away five tons of silver and 500 pounds of gold from this cathedral alone, but the Cossacks recovered most of the booty, and in gratitude then presented a solid silver chandelier weighing 900 pounds, with 46 branches, which hangs in the cupola.

### ONE OF THE WONDERS OF RUSSIA: THE BELL TOWER IN THE KREMLIN, WITH THE CATHEDRAL OF ARCHANGELS ON THE LEFT

The tower was built by Boris Goudonov, in order to give employment to the people at the time of the great Moscow famine (see text, pages 13 & 19). The tower contains 34 bells, the largest weighing 65 tons, which is clearly seen hanging in the center of the building (see also illustration, page 17). All the bells are large, one of the smaller being shown on page 18, and two of them are of silver. It was this same Boris Goudonov who reduced the peasants to serfdom, in which condition they remained until 1861. The Cathedral of Archangels (on the left) contains the tombs of all the Tsars and Grand Dukes until Peter the Great, the body of Ivan the Terrible resting beside that of his son, whom he slew with his own hand (see page 10).

## THE GREATEST BELL THAT MAN HAS EVER MADE

This huge bell was built by Boris Goudonov to hang in the bell tower, but when completed was found too heavy for the building to support. It was therefore hung on a platform outside the tower (travelers to Moscow in 1611 reported that twenty-four men were needed to swing the tongue), but a few years later a fire in the Kremlin destroyed the platform and the bell was broken. It was recast some years later, only to be again broken. A third time it was recast, this time even larger than before, but the water poured on it when it was red-hot, in another fire, caused it to crack. It fell again and remained buried for 100 years at the foot of the tower, until Emperor Nicholas I, in 1835, had it excavated and mounted, as shown in this picture. It is believed to weigh about 200 tons.

### THE GREATEST BELL IN SERVICE

This immense bell hangs in the bell tower and can be distinctly seen on page 15. It weighs 64 tons, or more than twice as much as the biggest bell of western Europe (see page 18), and was cast after the retreat of Napoleon from Moscow from some of the old bells. It is beautifully decorated with portraits of the Emperor Alexander I and his wife, Elizabeth, and of his mother and brothers. It is rung only a few times a year, at Christmas and Easter and on the Tsar's birthday. The man shown in the picture is standing exactly in the center of the bell, of which this is probably the first photograph made in the belfry.

### ONE OF THE 34 SMALLER BELLS IN THE BELL TOWER AT MOSCOW

It compares very favorably with the biggest bells of western Europe. The largest bell outside of Russia is the Emperor Bell, in the Cologne Cathedral in Germany, which weighs 27 tons, and the Great Bell in St. Paul's Cathedral, weighing 18 tons. Big Peter, in the York Cathedral, weighs only 11 tons, or no more than the broken fragment from the Queen of Bells, shown on page 16.

THE RICHEST AND MOST CELEBRATED MONASTERY IN MOSCOW:
MONASTERY OF MIRACLES (CHUDOV)

Here the ambassador of the Tatar Khan, to whom Moscow paid tribute for nearly 300 years, stabled his horses; but when the wife of the Khan was cured of an illness by Alexis, head (metropolitan) of the Russian church, she made a gift of the land to the church. Alexis then founded this monastery, whose buildings, like all other buildings in the Kremlin, have been rebuilt many times. The library contains several hundred valuable manuscripts on parchment, some of them dating from the thirteenth century. The utensils of gold and silver are priceless. It is still customary for parents to bring their children to the shrine to be blessed before they are put into school. At the time of Catherine II the monastery had 19,000 male serfs attached to it.

and the most appalling famine that ever devastated the capital of a nation. "Men were entrapped into dwellings, and killed and eaten. Pies made of human flesh were openly sold in the market. One hundred and twenty-seven thousand corpses remained for days unburied in the streets, and an eyewitness relates that 500,000 persons were carried off by the awful visitation."

## THE CATHEDRAL OF OUR SAVIOUR BEHIND THE GOLDEN GATES

This little church, built during the seventeenth century, was originally the private chapel of the Tsars. It is surmounted by twelve gilded cupolas, of which eleven may be seen in part in the photograph. The most treasured relic in the church is a sacred icon (holy picture), said to have been brought to Moscow by Princess Sophia Palaeologus, the heiress to Constantinople, who married Ivan III in 1472 (see page 7). With Sophia came a number of priests, who brought from Constantinople as many holy relics as they had been able to save when the city fell before Mohammed. The ground within the Kremlin walls is so sacred in Russian eyes that many remain uncovered while passing the cathedrals. Note the boy and two men on the right.

A VERY COMMON SIGHT IN RUSSIA: A DEVOUT RUSSIAN STOPPING TO CROSS HIMSELF AS HE PASSES A SHRINE

**A PRIEST AND HIS WIFE: MOSCOW**

The Russian clergy are divided into two classes—the black priests and the white priests. The white clergy are the parochial priests and are allowed to marry—in fact, must marry—but only once, while the black clergy live in monasteries and are celibates.

Anarchy continued. No one could agree as to who should be the Tsar. Amid the divided camps it was easy for the Polish king to overrun the country and to seize Moscow, from which he actually reigned. So exhausted was Russia that the empire seemed crumbling to pieces before the attacks of Swede, Turk, and Pole. But in this hour of adversity the Russian church, as during the centuries of Tatar rule, alone refused to submit, and in her monastery fortresses kept alive the spirit of resistance until a butcher called Minin and a prince, Pojarski, started a revival of the masses so violent that in a few months every Pole was swept out of Russia. But Moscow for perhaps the tenth time was burned to the ground.

TWO GUARDIANS OF THE KREMLIN: MOSCOW

All government officials, high and low, all school teachers, professors in universities, postmasters, etc., wear uniforms; in fact, it is calculated that one Russian in ten wears a uniform his whole life long.

At the Grand National Assembly which followed, and in which princes and peasants participated, Michael Romanov was chosen Tsar. Thus the present dynasty, which has brought stability, immense growth, and enormous power to Russia, was founded six years after the founding of Jamestown, Virginia, and only seven years before the Pilgrim fathers landed at Plymouth, Massachusetts.

PETER THE GREAT

Among the colossal figures that loom up above the dead level of humanity as a great mountain towers above the plain, history offers no better example than Peter the Great, Russia's remarkable ruler at the close of the seventeenth and during the beginning of the eighteenth century. He found Russia an all but barbaric nation;

RUSSIAN MOTHERS MAKING THE ROUND OF THE HOLY PLACES IN THE KREMLIN
They will press baby's lips to the sacred icons and relics regardless of how many have preceded them. Some of the bones are black with age, and the millions of caresses have formed a brown crust over some of the holy pictures.

he left it on the highroad to civilization and one of the earth's greatest powers.

He was born as rich as Midas, with the silver spoon of plenty in his mouth; but he lived as poor as a hermit, and toiled with hand as well as with brain that his country might come out of its barbaric stupor and into civilized activity. He justified his savage treatment of his people by saying that it was only through such methods that he was able to "dress his herd of animals like men;" and yet he lived with them and shared their toil when Russia's welfare was in the balance.

A very remarkable man was Peter the Great—a queer combination of autocrat and democrat, as austere as a monk: when Duty called and as self-indulgent as Bacchus when Pleasure beckoned.

Peter was born in Moscow in 1672. At his election to the throne, ten years later, he saw one of his uncles dragged from the palace and butchered by a savage mob, and his mother's beloved mentor and his own best friend (who had probably given him his thirst for knowledge) torn from his restraining grasp and hacked to pieces. As a youth he cared little who ruled his empire, so long as he was left undisturbed in his pastimes of shipbuilding, sailing, drilling, and fighting sham battles.

A disastrous campaign against the Turks and an attempt to capture Azov, which failed, simply aroused the latent forces in the great ruler, and he immediately sent to Austria and Prussia for sappers, miners, engineers, and carpenters, whom he took with him to the forests of the Don, where they constructed scores of vessels for his "sea caravan," with which he proposed to drive out the Turks from Azov. He himself lived in a hut in the woods and worked like a slave during this time, and when his galley flotilla started it was under the command of "Captain Peter Aleksyeevich" in the galley *Principum*, which he had built with his own hands. His expedition was successful—Azov was captured.

But after his victory Peter foresaw that he could not stand out single-handed against the Turks permanently; so he sent a deputation of nearly three hundred persons, including nobles, generals, merchants, and interpreters, to western Europe to ask support for his cause. He himself accompanied the embassy incognito: but soon, becoming impatient with the progress such a large party could make, he abandoned it and traveled alone, visiting Germany, Holland, England, France, and Austria.

Wherever he went he was indefatigable in learning new arts and gathering new ideas. In the factories he worked unknown with his own hands until they became hard and callous—in gun-making at Konigsberg, at shipbuilding in Holland, at manufacturing in general in England, and as an engraver in Amsterdam.

## PETER'S VISIT TO LONDON

The following story is told of Peter's visit to London:

"When the Tsar visited London, in 1698, he was much gazed at by the populace, and on one occasion was upset by a porter who pushed against him with his load. Lord Carmarthen, who was in attendance, fearing there would be a pugilistic encounter, turned angrily to the man and said, 'Don't you know this is the Tsar?' 'Tsar!' replied the man, with his tongue in his cheek; 'we are all Tsars here.'"*

Peter was starting from Vienna to Venice to learn the art of navigation more thoroughly when he was recalled to Moscow to put down an incipient revolution. He "had 2,000 hanged or broken on the wheel and 5,000 beheaded." Then he took up his work of establishing reforms, "the knout and the axe being the accompaniment of every reforming edict."

In these reforms he followed the ideal of the modern Japanese, showing no sentimental predilection for any one country, but borrowing with impartiality the best that each had to offer. Some of the things that worked well with the people of Western Europe were unsuited to

---

*This was ten years after the peaceful revolution in England. Already the main principles of English government, Macaulay says, "had been engraven on the hearts of Englishmen during 400 years. That, without the consent of the representatives of the nation, no legislative act could be passed, no tax imposed, no regular soldiery kept up; that no man could be imprisoned, even for a day, by the arbitrary will of the sovereign; that no tool of power could plead the royal command as a justification for violating any right of the humblest subject, were held, both by Whigs and Tories, to be fundamental laws of the realm."

These words of the brilliant historian make us realize the political backwardness of Russia, and of every other continental power of Europe at that time, as compared with England.

**LITTLE RUSSIANS IN MOSCOW**

The Russians have never believed in corporal punishment or laying violent hands on a child, and in this respect are generations ahead of England or the United States. Punishment of any kind is disapproved as likely to break a child's spirit and spoil his character.

Russia; but Peter made the man to fit the coat and not the coat to fit the man.

One of his first orders was that the beards of Russian officials should go; and, although the masses would have thought beheading little more shocking to their ideals, the beards went, as evidence that the old order was changing. Men were ordered to change their dress, women to discard their veils, and intimately personal affairs were reformed as well as public matters. The power of the clergy, who had constantly opposed his plans, was broken by the replacing of the patriarchate with a synod whose members were absolutely dependent upon the Tsar. He founded schools, built up a powerful army, and had the virtue of economy.

Peter foresaw the future of Siberia and of the great Amur River Valley and sought to develop both. He wanted a palace from whose window he could look out upon Europe, and he got it by building a city in a vast marsh. Forty thousand men were drafted annually to get logs from the forests and drive them as piling to make a foundation for his capital. Imagination staggers when trying to comprehend the vastness of the undertaking; but Petrograd stands as the twentieth-century fulfillment of his ideals in city-building.

SCHOOLBOYS AND PRIEST: MOSCOW

Many of the people met in Russia objected to the camera, thinking it had detective purposes, but the kindly old priest in this picture, who was teaching his boys Russian history by showing them the historic places and souvenirs of the Kremlin, when he saw that we were anxious to obtain a photograph of his party, without a word or any hint from us voluntarily lined the boys up against a wall and bade them keep motionless until the camera had clicked. However, the photograph obtained before his assistance was given proved more effective.

At the age of 53 Peter sacrificed his life to save a peasant woman and her child from drowning (see page 66).

## NAPOLEON IN MOSCOW

The taking of Moscow by Napoleon, its subsequent destruction, and the retreat of his army constitute one of the most thrilling pages in the annals of war. It was on the 14th of September, 1812, that the golden minarets and starry domes of the great city first met the gaze of the French army. "All this is yours," exclaimed the great chieftain, and a mighty shout swept over his army from front rank to rear guard, like a great billow over a sea.

The day before the Russians had evacuated the city and the way of the French was unopposed. But when they arrived they were chagrined to find that the 300,000 inhabitants had left, and that only the liberated prisoners, the rabble, and the feeble had remained behind. Napoleon himself occupied the Kremlin on the 15th, and that very night, while he was waiting to receive a deputation of notables, who sent in their stead a deputation of rich *raskolnik* merchants (as dissenters from the Greek Catholic Church are called), fires were lit in all parts of the city by Russians chosen for the work. Fanned by a high wind, the flames quickly spread into a great conflagration. The hospitals, containing 20,000 wounded, soon fell prey

THE GREAT CANNON: KREMLIN, MOSCOW

The Tsar's cannon, or the king of cannons, weighs a little more than forty tons, and is seventeen and two-thirds feet in length. It was long considered the largest cannon in the world, and has never been fired. Probably heavier cannons than this are being fired this very day in the European war.

to the fire, and the spectacle was one of infinite horror.

After the fire came the orgy of pillage. Soldiers, sutlers, galley slaves, and prostitutes, unmindful of the horrible sufferings of those who had been burned, but in whose bodies yet remained the spark of life, began to ply their nefarious trade. Some clothed themselves in the richest of silks and the finest of furs. Even the galley slaves concealed their rags under the most splendid court dresses. Cellars were broken open, and a saturnalia of drunkenness added to the horrors.

"Palaces and temples," writes Karamzin, "monuments of art and miracles of luxury, the remains of past ages and those which had been the creation of yesterday, the tombs of ancestors and the nursery cradles of the present generation, were indiscriminately destroyed; nothing was left of Moscow save the remembrance of the city and the deep resolution to avenge its fate."

THE MOST IMPRESSIVE MONUMENT IN RUSSIA TO THE DEFEAT OF NAPOLEON;
A ROW OF 895 CANNONS CAPTURED FROM HIS ARMY DURING RETREAT

Almost every gun bears the initial "N" surrounded by a laurel wreath. At least twenty thousand horses were required to drag these guns and the ammunition for them.

## THEY DIED LIKE FLIES ON THE COMING OF WINTER

The Russians flatly refused to consider peace proposals at such a juncture, and declared that there was no use to suggest an armistice, for the Russian army was at that moment preparing to resume the offensive.

For a month the Great Corsican lingered amid the cinders of the city, but on the 19th of October he left, with his 120,000 men, a vast amount of plunder, and a great horde of camp followers. He was barely well under way when a winter of unusual severity set in. The thermometer dropped to 18 degrees, the wind blew furiously, and a driving, blinding snow made the march a discipline-breaking, heart-rending ordeal. Many fell by the wayside and found a snowy grave; others crawled on, with nothing to eat or to drink, frost-bitten and groaning with pain.

Discipline disappeared completely; no soldier obeyed his officer. Disbanded, the troops spread themselves right and left in search of food, and, as the horses fell one by one, they fought over the mangled carcasses and

### ANOTHER VIEW OF THE LONG LINE OF GUNS CAPTURED FROM NAPOLEON

Moscow represented to the Russians everything dearest in their national, religious, and commercial life, and yet all Russians—priests, merchants, peasants, and soldiers—joined to sacrifice it when Napoleon's invasion threatened to reduce Russia to subjection. Napoleon had counted on the city's rich stores of grain and furs and on the thousands of horses there to replenish his army and to afford comfortable quarters during the winter, but the Russians preferred to starve and freeze through a Russian winter if that was the only way to beat Napoleon (see page 27).

**FEEDING THE PIGEONS IN THE GREAT RED SQUARE:
IN FRONT OF BASIL'S CATHEDRAL (SEE PAGE 75)**

The square was the scene of public executions when the Tsars reigned from Moscow. Another view of this square is given on page 11.

devoured them raw. Many remained by the bivouac fires, allowing the insensibility of cold to creep over them and usher them into that long bivouac that knows no waking until the roll is called beyond the river. They died like flies on the coming of winter, and when Napoleon crossed the Berezina the wretched remnant of his once-powerful army was nearly annihilated. A Russian account says that 36,000 bodies were found in that river alone.

Of the half a million men with whom Napoleon had gone forward to break the Russian power, 125,000 were slain in battle, 132,000 died from fatigue, hunger, and cold, and 193,000 were taken prisoners. Only about 40,000 escaped the general wreck, which was the greatest military catastrophe of history or tradition.

## FREEING THE SERFS

Perhaps the greatest single act of any ruler in all history was that of Tsar Alexander II in freeing the 50 million serfs of Russia in 1861. Not only did he release more than half the people of his empire from bondage, but he also bought 350 million acres of land from the land-owners and turned it over to the villages, to be held as communal property and to be paid for by the villages in installments running 50 years.

This act of Alexander, taken so shortly before Lincoln's Emancipation Proclamation, makes our freeing of the negro look small in comparison. Alexander's ukase affected 50 million bondmen, nearly as many persons as are now living in the 12 most populous States of the Union, as follows: New York, Pennsylvania, Illinois, Ohio, Texas, Massachusetts, Missouri, Michigan, Indiana, Georgia, New Jersey, and California. Lincoln's proclamation affected less than four million; Alexander's ukase affected more than half of his country's population; Lincoln's proclamation directly touched less than an eighth of our population.

While this achievement in agrarian reform helped the serfs a good deal, it did not accomplish all they had expected; indeed, it fell far short of the relief they desired.

The peasants could not understand why it was that, having been born on the land, having tilled it from time immemorial, and having been its caretakers and the source of its value for centuries, they should be forced to pay for it. Many of their villages long groaned under the burden of paying for the communal property thus transferred to them at prices they had no part in fixing.

The ukase freeing the serfs gave them a communal form of government for their villages. They had had their legislative assemblies from immemorial antiquity, but it was not until the act of emancipation that the village community was withdrawn from the patrimonial jurisdiction of the land-owning nobility and endowed with self-government. Each village is a miniature pure democracy, where even representative government would be regarded as too remote. The heads of the houses in a village meet in free consultation on the basis of "one man, one vote." This true democracy, within an autocratic monarchy, divides the lands to be cultivated, disciplines its members, provides relief for the needy, and buys fire-engines and agricultural machinery. It selects a head man, who is the president of all village meetings. Another official selected is the pole man, who goes through the village tapping on the windows to warn the people that a village meeting is about to be held.

Nothing is done until the villagers in meeting approve it. For instance, no one can begin to mow hay until the village meeting says so. The village lands are apportioned out, each male member of a family getting a strip; and these are not located together, thus preventing any family from getting more than its share of the best land. Sometimes there is a redivision every ten years, and sometimes oftener. Sometimes strips are 10 feet wide and sometimes 200—a strange effect in harvest time, when the land looks like a piece of grandmother's homemade rag carpet. Hay is usually made by the whole community and divided into a number of piles corresponding to the number of men, and these are assigned by lot.

A POOR MAN'S FUNERAL PROCESSION IN MOSCOW

Russia is noted as a land of elaborate funerals. This picture shows a procession at a funeral of a poor person, and many a poor family almost bankrupts itself in order to give a proper outward show of its sorrow. All the mourners walk, although several carriages may follow with no one riding in them. The funeral car usually is drawn by six mantled horses, each led by a groomsman in white uniform. The services at the church are long and impressive.

## A RURAL-LIVING PEOPLE

Few nations have such a great percentage of their population living on the soil and by the soil as Russia. Where England and Wales have 78 per cent of their people living amid urban surroundings, the United States 47 per cent, Germany 43 per cent, and France 42 per cent, only 15 per cent of Russia's people have left the soil. Of the typical thousand of population, 771 are peasants, 107 are burgesses, 66 are natives of the wildtribe order, 23 are Cossacks, 15 are nobles, 5 belong to the clergy, 5 are privileged burgesses, and 8 are unclassified.

Being preëminently a land of agriculturists, lands are in Russia what stocks and bonds

**WORKMEN IN THE KREMLIN: MOSCOW**
Big and sturdy, they are swinging along with the easy and springing step characteristic of the powerful Russian race.

are in England—the principal field for investment. The great Black Forest region is one of the most fertile on the face of the earth; its soil is from 3 to 10 feet deep, and its agricultural possibilities match anything that may be found in Iowa or the Dakotas.

Thus the geographical handicap of early years—that wide, flat plain over which the armed hosts could drive without hindrance, burning and butchering—is now Russia's greatest asset.

With the bulk of its crops raised by the peasantry, employing the most primitive means of farming, Russia is still able to produce a very large proportion of the world's food supply. In 1913 it gave to civilization nearly a fourth of its wheat, fully a fourth of its oats, a third of its barley, and more than half of its rye. The Empire

ONE OF THE MOST HISTORIC GROUP OF
BUILDINGS IN MOSCOW: CONVENT NOVO-DEVITSCHY

Within the shelter of the massive walls of this convent more than one of the royal widows, sisters, or daughters have taken refuge. Here was imprisoned the ambitious and gifted sister of Peter the Great, Sophia, who ruled when he was a boy, and who did her best, according to Peter, to put him out of the way, so that she might become permanent Empress. In front of the Russian monasteries and convents there is usually a little sentry box, where a nun or priest is always present to receive the copper which the passing peasant may volunteer.

in that year had a wheat crop 200 million bushels greater than that of the United States, an oats crop offsetting our own, a barley crop three times as great as ours, and a rye crop 25 times the size of ours.

But for our tremendous crop of corn, approximating 2½ billion bushels, the United States would have to yield first place to Russia as a grain producer.

## FUTURE POSSIBILITIES

But what Russia is as a producer of the world's staple foodstuffs is nothing as compared

A PEDDLER OF PICTURES OF THE RUSSIAN SAINTS

with what it may be. That the acreage can be enormously increased, any one who has traveled through Russia can very well understand. But let us assume that the acreage will stand still, and that at some future date the Russian farmer, with his naturally rich and comparatively new land, can duplicate what the German farmer, with his naturally poor and long-used

A NUN IN MOSCOW

land, is now doing in the matter of per-acre yield.

Russia then would be able to give the world three-eighths of its present wheat supply, two-thirds of its present oats crop, five-sixths of its present barley harvest, and nearly half a billion bushels more than its present yield of rye.

### ONE OF THE MODERN SHRINES IN THE CITY OF MOSCOW

It is situated in a public square in the business section of the city. The little houses on the left are market stalls. The electric car was made in the United States. The routes of the electric cars in Moscow are indicated by large numerals carried conspicuously in front of the car, making it easy for the traveler to find his way about the city. Note the double-headed eagle on the columns in front of the shrine. Ever since the Prince of Moscow Ivan III, married the heiress of the last Constantine, the Russian royal house has used the double-headed eagle, which for one thousand years had been the emblem of the Byzantine Empire, and Russians have dreamed of becoming the heirs to Constantinople (see page 7).

SCENE IN A CLOTH MARKET IN THE JEWS' BAZAAR, SHOWING THE PICTORIAL SIGNS USED BY THE MERCHANTS IN ADVERTISING THEIR WARES

Very few of the people can read and write, and consequently pictures are the usual method of advertising. The letters in the name of a restaurant are written in green and yellow, the top part of the letters being green to represent eating and the lower part yellow to represent drinking.

As a stock-raising country Russia stands out as having more horses than any other nation on earth, with the United States as its nearest rival. It has 35 million as compared with our 24 million; it has 80 million sheep as compared with our 50 million, and 51 million cattle as compared with our 59 million. With the government spending money with lavish hand to bring into Russia the best blood that is to be found in the stock of Europe and America, the result is showing in its horses, its cattle, and its sheep.

SHOPS FOR THE SALE OF SACRED ICONS—THAT IS, REPRESENTATIONS
OF CHRIST, OF ANGELS, AND SAINTS: MOSCOW

The icons are the symbols of the saints and of God. In every Russian home, in every room in your hotel, in the railway waiting-rooms, everywhere there is an icon. It is not proper to sit with one's back to it. It consecrates the home, and is a reminder to the Russian that "God is in the midst"—not locked up in the church, but always present. The representations of Christ, of angels, and of saints are given in relief or mosaic or are painted.

## EDUCATIONAL CONDITIONS

Russia has the largest proportion of illiterates of any civilized country, although in recent years conditions have been improving. The latest authoritative information, that for 1908, shows that out of every 1,000 of population only 211 can read and write. How much progress has been made, however, in the work of introducing general education is revealed by the fact that the census of the early nineties showed that only 50 out of every 1,000 were literates.

Illiteracy is much more common among the women than among the men. In Russia as a whole there are 22 men who can read and write for every 10 women who are able to do so. In Siberia there are 38 literate males for every 10 literate females.

PEOPLE SEEN IN THE BAZAAR AT MOSCOW

The great variety of the races under the Russian flag is nowhere better illustrated than here. From all parts of Asia have come representatives of the different peoples, each wearing its native costume.

THESE HANDSOMELY GOWNED OFFICIALS ARE ATTENDANTS IN A MUSEUM

One takes your coat, another your hat, and a third your stick or umbrella, and each must be substantially remembered when you leave.

A RUSSIAN PRIEST, WITH HIS WIFE AND TWO CHILDREN, VISITING THE MUSEUM
"The clergy forms a caste apart; priests and deacons marry the daughters of priests and deacons, and it very often happens that an old priest on retiring passes his parish on to his son-in-law. The priest's wife brings with her a tradition of good housekeeping that has been handed down in the families of the clergy from generation to generation, made necessary by the poor salaries paid and the large families to provide for. The children are educated in special schools for the clergy, and if, as sometimes happens, the children do not follow their parent's profession, they often enter the government service as clerks or teachers." See H. W. Williams's book, "Russia of the Russians" (Scribners).

Some idea of the interest of the people at large in education is revealed by a comparison of school populations in Russia and the United States. With a population of 100 million, the total enrolment in the public and private schools of the United States in 1912 amounted to 19,218,000. With a population of 172 million, the total enrollment in all the schools in Russia,

### A COACHMAN IN MOSCOW

The drosky drivers wear padded coats that look like great wrappers round their bodies. The fatter they are the more prosperous and well-fed they are supposed to be, and consequently the more high-priced. The cab driver takes better care of his horse than he does of himself, and would prefer to go hungry than to have his horse starve. Many of these "hack" horses are as fine as the swellest turnout of the rich in America.

**A YOUNG RUSSIAN: MOSCOW**

Russia has the largest proportion of illiterates of any civilized country, although in recent years conditions have been improving (see page 40).

Besides their church duties, the priests teach in synodical schools, where they give lessons in church history and the catechism and in reading and writing Church Slavonic the language in which the church services are conducted.

including public and private, primary and higher schools, was 7,970,000, and there were 23 males for every 10 females in this enrollment.

A law was passed several years ago making general education compulsory, but the growth of the village schools notwithstanding has been much slower than its proponents had hoped to witness.

## THE POSITION OF WOMAN

Although women in general have received such little attention educationally, Russia lives up well to its reputation as a land of extremes in this regard, for Russia was the first country in Europe to establish a technical school for women. The first woman civil engineer in the world was a Russian, and as far back as 1859 a woman was admitted to the University of Petrograd.

The educated woman in Russia enjoys a position of freedom equal to that of any other country in the world. She is frequently found as owner and manager of large factories and estates; she gets her degrees at the universities along with men; she is given posts as teachers of all kinds, including professorships at men's universities, and she practices medicine and dentistry. There is a marked tendency to encourage her entering the legal profession, and the Constitutional Democrats in the Duma want to

**THIS SHRINE FACES ONE OF THE BUSIEST THOROUGHFARES OF MOSCOW**

The author watched scores of people pass it, the majority of whom uncovered or crossed themselves as they went by. Finally, seeing this dignified individual appear the author snapped the shutter as he took off his hat, but the gentleman had uncovered not out of respect to the shrine, but to mop his forehead, it being a frightfully hot summer day.

### A RUSSIAN GENTLEMAN PROSTRATED IN PRAYER BEFORE THE IBERIAN CHAPEL

This little chapel, which is hardly wider than the open doors, is one of the most holy shrines in Russia. The Emperor always stops here on his way to the Kremlin. Under the bright blue roof, which is studded with gilded stars, is an icon of the Virgin brought from Mt. Athos and supposed to have miraculous powers of healing and blessing. Every morning, in a carriage drawn by six horses, attended by priests and servants, it is carried to the houses of the sick, to weddings, to the blessing of a new house, or to inaugurate the special sale of a merchant. For these visits it receives various presents, sometimes as much as $50. Its appointments are scheduled months ahead. While it is on its round of visits an exact duplicate of the sacred picture reposes in its place. Hundreds of pilgrims and Muscovites stop each day to kiss it, to say a prayer, or burn a taper before it. When we passed the shrine one night, as late as 11 o'clock, there were over 100 men, women, and children waiting to see the original picture return from its tour and to receive its blessing as it was carried in by the priests.

### VIEW FROM AFAR OF THE CATHEDRAL OF OUR SAVIOR AND OF THE GATE THROUGH WHICH NAPOLEON FIRST ENTERED THE KREMLIN

This immense, beautifully proportioned white building, with its five golden domes glistening in the sun and standing out against a bright blue sky, is one of the memories which every visitor to Moscow will always cherish. The cathedral was built by popular subscriptions as a thanksgiving to God for the defeat of Napoleon's army (see also pages 49 and 80). All the materials used for the building are Russian, and all the work was by Russian architects, artists, and artisans.

### A NEAR VIEW OF THE WONDERFUL CATHEDRAL OF THE SAVIOUR

Its interior is a blaze of color (see page 80). Nearly seven thousand worshipers can find accommodations in it at one time. On Sundays the services are attended by so many men that women are wont to go on the other days of the week. This stately edifice, the magnificent cathedrals of St. Isaac's (see page 88), and the Church of the Resurrection (see page 81) were all erected within the last one hundred years, and are lasting monuments to the present religious spirit in Russia. No other Christian country within the last century has built three cathedrals, or even one, to equal these. It should be remembered, however, that the Russian church does not proselyte, whereas the Protestant and Roman Catholic churches have devoted hundreds of millions of dollars to foreign mission work.

## MOSCOW IN WINTER

When bleak, white winter settles over the City of Moscow her energies are caught and subdued by its might. All wheel traffic ceases, the streets become almost bare of pleasure strollers and all that moves without under the leaden, stinging sky moves hurriedly, with a definite goal in view, and takes the shortest course. Moscow lives under a reddened sun but for a short time each day. Only the cabman, with his dozen coats, a creature thick beyond imagination, cares to loiter chill afternoons and evenings out of doors.

admit her to the duties of jury service. When women teachers and professors have served 20 years they are entitled to retire on a government pension, and if they die and are survived by husbands, the pensions continue during their husbands' lives.

There are ten government universities in Russia, the largest that of Petrograd, with 10,364

### RUSSIA'S GREATEST RIVER, THE VOLGA, AT
### NIZHNI-NOVGOROD, 1,500 MILES FROM ITS MOUTH

Although as far from its mouth as Denver is from New York, Nizhni-Novgorod is still some 800 miles below the source of the Volga. In the upper reaches its depth is not more than a foot and a half, although its width is 600 feet. Special types of flat-bottomed boats make it navigable even there. Twenty years ago the sales at the annual fair, open only one month in summer, amounted to $100,000,000, but the development of railways is diverting this commerce elsewhere and the fair is losing much of its Asiatic character, and the river traffic, as on our own Mississippi, has greatly decreased. The fair grounds are the flats over which the cathedral towers on the left, between the Volga and Oka rivers.

students. The one at Moscow has 9,000 students, and the one at Kharkov 5,274. A popular university was established in 1909 at Moscow under a fund left by General Shaniavsky.

But with all these universities the average Russian is as illiterate as the statistics cited above show. We had numerous experiences revealing his illiteracy and his indisposition to confess it. On several occasions our guide had told our drosky driver, a different man each time, to take us to a certain store and had given him the street and number. He immediately set off and drove to the street, but continued driving slowly up that thoroughfare, looking

### LOOKING TOWARD THE WATER FRONT OF THE OLD
### CITY OF NIZHNI-NOVGOROD, FROM THE FAIR GROUNDS

The banks are crowded with river steamers and barges that have brought silks from Persia, great bales of cotton and madder from Bokhara, hides from Siberia, and oil from the Caspian. Behind are seen the domes and spires of several monasteries and churches. We visited one of the convents, where we found a beautiful garden with lovely walks beneath great trees. The gardens are tended by the nuns, who also work very industriously in embroidering vestments for the churches and patrons. We were present at vespers in the convent which was attended by 200 nuns, all dressed in blackest of robes and ugly black head-coverings, with long black veils, while the services were conducted by two priests in gorgeous, richly embroidered golden robes.

### A PORTER AT THE RAILWAY STATION, NIZHNI-NOVGOROD

This big fellow, over 6 feet 2 inches in height, with his long flaxen beard and blue eyes, is a good specimen of the Russian peasant. His father was a serf. Perhaps the greatest single act of any ruler in all history was that of Tsar Alexander II in freeing the 50 million serfs of Russia in 1861. He released from bondage more than half the people of his empire, nearly as many persons as are now living in the 12 most populous States of the Union. Lincoln's proclamation affected less than four million (see text, page 32).

### A WEALTHY TATAR MERCHANT WHO HAS JUST ARRIVED FOR THE GREAT ANNUAL FAIR AT NIZHNI-NOVGOROD
Note his tall boots, polished like a mirror, and his small skull-cap, which marks the Tatar.

## Young Russia   The Land of Unlimited Possibilities

### A BOAT ON THE VOLGA RIVER

On an ideal Sunday afternoon in midsummer we made an excursion to Sparrow Hill, in the suburbs of Moscow. From its summit we could see the beautiful Moskva River, fringed with trees and meadows, winding around the plain in which Moscow lies; but on the river not a single pleasure boat, not even a single canoe. The people of any other city of equal size in Germany, France, England, or America (Moscow has 1½ million) would have covered the river on such an afternoon with canoes and pleasure craft.

### A PRISONER: NIZHNI-NOVGOROD

### THERE ARE NOT AS MANY SHRINES AND CHAPELS IN NIZHNI-NOVGOROD AS IN MOSCOW

This one is by the station, and a laborer has lingered to offer his devotions and leave a kopeck before the Icon on the table; a representation of Christ in bronze and mosaic, protected from the weather by a glass frame. Note the candle burning behind the glass. The pictures accompanying this article, showing peasant and gentlemen at devotion, pages 6, 12, 20, 21, and 47, are actual snapshots. None of them were posed or planned; similar scenes may be seen every moment, everywhere in Russia. His religion is very real to the Russian, and his God is really omnipresent to him; he sees His Spirit everywhere, and everywhere acknowledges it with the sign of the cross and the words "Oh, Lord! have mercy," or "Glory be to Thee, Oh, Lord!" (see also page 40).

Young Russia   The Land of Unlimited Possibilities

THIS MAN IS TYPICAL OF THE THOUSANDS OF BIG MUSCULAR
PEASANTS WHO THRONG NTZHNI-NOVGOROD DURING THE FAIR

**A RUSSIAN BRIDEGROOM AT NIZHNI-NOVGOROD PAYING FOR HIS BOOTBLACK**
He wore a bright crimson silk blouse, while his bride's dress was of somber black.

A MOUJIK LOOKING FOR WORK: NIZHNI-NOVGOROD

THIS WOMAN IS WEARING STRAW SANDALS; A LUXURY, FOR MOST PEASANT WOMEN GO BAREFOOTED

back at us occasionally for further directions. Finally he reached the end of the street and, to our surprise, turned and slowly retraced the ground traversed, asking us by signs, for we understood no Russian, which store we wished to visit. We finally realized that the drosky driver could not even read figures, the numbers on the doors. It was then that we fully under-

PEASANTS: NIZHNI-NOVGOROD

stood the necessity for the pictorial rather than written signs before many of the stores, more especially in the poor sections. These signs show coats, hats, shoes, caps, trousers, sausages, etc. The restaurants even have particular colors in their signs, something like our barbers' poles. The name is written in green and yellow—the top part of the letters green

**TWO ILLUSTRATIONS OF THE UNIQUE TYPE OF CART USED THROUGHOUT RUSSIA**
These carts carry about 1,100 pounds each, and are so built that they will negotiate the muddiest roads. The upper picture (in the old fortress at Nizhni-Novgorod) shows the manner in which the cart may be tilted and easily emptied. The lower picture depicts the peculiar and universal Russian yoke.

**A VODKA SHOP (SALOON) IN NIZHNI-NOVGOROD**

Every dram shop in the Russian Empire is now said to be closed. "The abolition of the sale of intoxicants in Russia represents the greatest prohibition victory of the age. With one dash of the pen one-sixth of the earth's surface and one-tenth of its population went 'dry.' Heretofore vodka-drinking has been the curse of the Russian masses" (see text).

**THE CARRIAGE OF AN ARISTOCRAT IN PETROGRAD**

Russia is the home of mettlesome horses and of inimitable horsemanship. The wiry, enduring horse of the steppes has been crossed with the larger-boned, dragoon-mount of East Prussian and Silesian breeders. The resulting strain is powerful, clean-limbed, speedy. Horsemanship is an important part of the Russian gentleman's education. Elegance of carriage on horseback and admirable driving are more often seen in the Tsar's domain than in any other part of Europe.

and the lower part yellow. We were told that the green stood for eating and the yellow for drinking, so that at a glance the most ignorant might recognize a restaurant or a café (p. 39).

**A WELL-PAID RULER**

The Tsar of Russia is a well-paid ruler. He receives the revenues from the Russian crown

### A GROUP OF RUSSIAN COSSACKS

The Cossacks are the world's foremost rough riders. Vast areas of land were many years ago set aside for them by the government in return for their military services. These lands, totaling 146,000,000 acres—105,000,000 of these arable and 10,000,000 under forest—are among the richest in Russia. They have been apportioned on the basis of 81 acres per person, leaving about a third in reserve. The men, in return for this bounty of the government, are required to give 20 years of service—one-third active—to the army, furnishing all their own equipment, including horses, except arms and ammunition. Their rich lands give them large incomes, and they are better educated than any other like body of the general population.

lands, and their area is equal to that of one-third of the United States—aggregating more than a million square miles. If you were to take all of the land in the United States lying east of the Mississippi you would still need several States like Massachusetts to make up an area equal to that of the domain whose revenues are the property of the Tsar. His total income

### THIS STATUE IN PETROGRAD COMMEMORATES THE ACT OF HEROISM WHICH RESULTED IN THE DEATH OF PETER THE GREAT

Peter had been confined to the house for some days with a high fever. and one afternoon, in spite of the protest of his physician, went for a walk along the Neva. Seeing a woman and child who were attempting to cross the river on the young ice break through and in danger of drowning, without a moment's hesitation he plunged into the water to their rescue and saved both. But the chill was so serious that it aggravated his complaint and caused his immediate death (see page 23).

THE FIRST AND LAST IMPRESSION OF PETROGRAD IS THE NOBLE
GOLDEN DOME OF ST. ISAAC'S WATCHING OVER THE CITY (SEE PAGE 90)

THE RIVER IN WINTER IS COVERED WITH
ICE SO THICK THAT TRAM CARS RUN OVER IT

One must admire the Russian for the energy he has displayed in making a seaport of Petrograd, and in developing a commerce for it almost as great as that of the city of Baltimore. The city is built on a marsh as far north as the southern tip of Greenland. Its waters freeze hard before Thanksgiving and do not melt before the end of April, and all its commerce must pass in or out by a canal from Kronstadt, 23 feet deep and 17 1/2 miles long. "With all its geographic greatness Russia is about as poor in natural outlets to the world as the smallest of the countries of the earth. Holland could be hidden in the vast reaches of the Russian plain, almost as a needle in a haystack, and yet Amsterdam alone does more international business than all the seaports of Russia together" (see pages 3–4).

**CIRCASSIANS PROMENADING IN THE PARK AT SPARROW HILL: MOSCOW**

There are as many different races under the Russian flag as there are in the British Empire. These men are Circassians from the Caucasus Mountains east of the Black Sea. They come of a proud and fearless people, noted for their love of country, their chivalry and their splendid physique. Though few in number, they resisted subjugation for many years, and it was not until 1864 that the Russians finally subdued them. These men are wearing their picturesque racial costume, a richly colored robe, adorned with a belt of cartridges.

RUSSIAN BOYS VISITING THE GLORIES OF THE KREMLIN, MOSCOW

They are wearing the characteristic Russian blouse, which is gaily colored and the fasion for all males in Russia, young and old.

"Above Moscow there is nothing but the Kremlin, above the Kremlin nothing but the sky," runs a Russian saying. Here have come the Czars to their baptisms, their coronations, their marriages, and their burials. It is the stronghold of Imperial Moscow, a city within a city. Its Imperial Quarter comprises four or five squares, two palaces, a treasury, the seat of the military Governor, several monuments, three cathedrals, many churches and chapels, three convents, barracks, an arsenal, and a palace of justice.

ranges around 30 million dollars a year. Several years ago the imperial treasurer made a report on the Tsar's private bank account, in which is said to have occurred the following passage:

"Your Majesty need have no fear of ever coming to suffer the stings of poverty. Financially you are solvency itself. With one hand you could buy out the American multimillionaires, Morgan and Rockerfeller, and still have sufficient to talk business with Baron Rothschild." The story goes that the flippancy of his treasurer very much displeased the Tsar. Whether the incident be an apocryphal tale or a true account of an actual happening, the royal banker told the truth if he wrote what is attributed to him.

When stern old Alexander gave orders to the tutors to the then heir to the throne, he said to them: "Neglect nothing that can make my

**WORKMEN REPAIRING A PAVEMENT IN THE CITY OF MOSCOW**

Laborers, instead of wearing the white uniform customary in our cities, wear the universal Russian blouse. These are usually gaily colored, bright red, yellow, blue, green, etc. The heavy boots, shown in the picture, while perhaps uncomfortable during the few days of summer heat, are very serviceable during the other months of the year, as Russian roads are notoriously poor.

son truly a man." Nicholas II, the present Tsar, was born in 1868, and ascended the throne in early manhood. At the age of 24 he made a tour of the Far East, visiting China and Japan. He returned to St. Petersburg by way of Siberia, and is the only Tsar who ever visited his Asiatic dominions.

Tsar Nicholas is noted for having made an effort to secure the peace of the world by a general conference. In his famous rescript of

CAMERA-SHY BUT NOT ALTOGETHER UNWILLING

August 24, 1898, he declared that the time had arrived for throwing off the crushing economic burdens entailed by the armed peace of Europe, and that the way to do so seemed to be through a conference of all the peace-loving States and the focusing of all their efforts in behalf of the noble idea of the triumph of universal peace over the elements of trouble and discord. His call resulted in the Hague peace conference of 1899, with 26 governments represented, and

## THREE GYPSIES ON THE STREETS OF MOSCOW

They are fond of extavagant colors, and, like all gypsies, wear necklaces of coins which have been heirlooms for many generations. Some of the old coins are worth many times their weight in gold.

Young Russia    The Land of Unlimited Possibilities

BOYS OF A WELL-TO-DO FAMILY IN THE STREETS OF NIZHNI-NOVGOROD,
IN WHICH CITY RUSSIA'S GREAT FAIR HAS BEEN HELD EACH YEAR SINCE 1817

A RUSSIAN GIRL IN MOSCOW, WITH A GLIMPSE OF THE UNIVERSITY TO HER LEFT.
THE SHAWL IS AS UBIQUITOUS HERE AS THE MANTILLA IN SPANISH-AMERICA.
TO THE MASSES THE QUESTION OF MILLNERY IS PURELY ACADEMIC.

### THE CATHEDRAL OF ST. BASIL'S: MOSCOW

St. Basil's is remarkable for its bizarre outlines and the gaudy color of its exterior. The interior is very disappointing, being divided into eleven small and gloomy chapels, which resemble dungeons. In this they are unlike the typical Russian church, which is elaborately adorned in gold and other rich colors.

### FORTH TO THE HARVEST

In Russia one may see in the harvest fields women wearing needlework on their dresses that many an American society woman would be proud to possess. Between rearing the biggest families in the world, keeping house and lending a willing hand in the field when needed, the Russian peasant woman finds time in the long winters to express her love of the beautiful through a needle.

### A RUSSIAN REBECCA AT THE WELL

This picture well typifies the pastoral civilization of peasant Russia. Nothing is bought by a peasant that he can fashion for himself, for rubles are few and far between with him. What little they buy is usually obtained in trade, and very many of them handle less money in a year than the average American workman handles in a day.

# The Russian People in 1914

### WHERE RACE SUICIDE HAS NEVER BEEN HEARD OF

The Russians are noted for their fecundity. In spite of the fact that the science of preventative medicine is a sealed book to the masses and their death-rate therefore very high, they still show a greater excess of births over deaths than any other leading country—with 17 per thousand of population, as compared with 11.3 in Germany; 10.1 in Italy; about 7.5 in the United States; and 0.9 in France. Without immigration, and in spite of emigration, the population has increased 90 per cent in forty years, which means that it will probably reach 267,000,000 by 1952.

A FORTUNE TELLER AND HIS ASSISTANT, NIZHNI-NOVGOROD

### THE CATHEDRAL OF THE SAVIOR: MOSCOW

This great structure, erected as Moscow's thank-offering for her deliverance from Napoleon, and completed in 1883 at a cost of seven million dollars, is regarded by artists and architects alike as Russia's masterpiece in cathedral architecture. The effects obtained by the blending of red, white and grey marbles, with gold and gilt bronze, quite beggar description. Russia's greatest artists contributed to its mural decoration. There are no seats and no organ, and high and low, rich and poor stand alike throughout the service. Beyond the door of the consecrated chamber behind the altar no woman's foot may tread.

## THE CHURCH OF THE RESURRECTION AT PETROGRAD

A magnificent edifice with wonderful, parti–colored minarets and an interior that has borrowed all of the priceless metals, gems and marbles for its beauty. It cost twenty million rubles (ten million dollars), contributed by the Russian people, to commemorate the murdered "Liberator of the Serfs and Friend of Finland," Alexander II. The church stands over the site where he was assassinated by a bomb-thrower in 1881.

### A SMALL FARMER'S TEAM IN RUSSIA

The wagons and harness used by the Russian peasant farmer are rudely fashioned. The women work in the field as well as the men. The whole family, little and big, each must do his part toward keeping the wolf from the door.

that of 1907, with 44 nations participating. Most of the Powers regarded the plan as altogether visionary, but the present permanent Court of Arbitration is largely the result of the Tsar's initiative. Of all the Great Powers, the United States was the only one unreservedly in favor of disarmament.

It is the irony of fate that the ruler who called the conference has had to participate in two of the bloodiest wars of all history in the sixteen short years that have elapsed since the issuance of his call in behalf of the world's peace.

The government of Russia is a limited monarchy under an autocratic Tsar, whose official title is "Emperor and Autocrat of all the Russias." The Tsar's autocratic power was theoretically surrendered in 1905 and 1906, when he created the Duma and the Council of State, corresponding in a measure to our own House of Representatives and Senate, without whose sanction no law shall go into effect. The Duma is made up of elected members who are chosen by electoral colleges instead of direct votes, and the peasants have scant representation in these electoral bodies. The Council of State is composed of representatives of the Tsar, of the provinces, of the church, of the educational institutions, of industry and commerce, and of the nobility. One-half of its members are appointees of the Tsar.

THE THRONE ROOM IN THE OLD IMPERIAL PALACE:
THE TEREM, IN THE KREMLIN, MOSCOW

The Terem dates from about 1626. It is a rather small palace of five stories all the rooms being decorated in gorgeous coloring.

## THE GERMANS CONTROLLED THE GREATEST SHARE OF RUSSIA'S FOREIGN BUSINESS

Before the outbreak of the present war Germany was walking away with the lion's share of Russia's foreign business. Many English statesmen had noted this and had commented upon it. At Chelyabinsk and Vladivostok Great Britain was getting a bad third, with Germany first and America second. One writer declares that the only thing he noticed in which Great Britain was ahead was sauce, and complained that the British sought to capture Russian trade with catalogues printed in English. Moscow merchants frequently asserted that England would not trade in as sensible a manner as the Germans, because they expected everybody to read and speak English, because they quoted all prices in pounds and shillings, because they never knew a freight rate, and because they always had to "consult the firm." On the other hand, these merchants declared, "the Germans know everything, solve every problem, and meet every emergency." Germany established branch banks in Russia, and could give from 12 to 18 months' credit to Russian firms, and credit the Russian tradesman always asks.

### A DUTCH FISHERMAN AND HIS FAMILY

On the island of Marken, in the Zuider Zee, the bloomer costumes of the adults, together with their wooden shoes and derby hats, have a unique appearance. Their costumes differ somewhat from the dress of the mainland peasants.

German, until the war, was a much more necessary language for a traveler in Russia than French or English. There were many German shop-keepers, and the chambermaids and waiters of the big hotels all spoke German.

While Russia's foreign trade has been regarded as full of potentialities, measured by population standards it is exceedingly small. With a population 70 per cent larger than that of the United States, its imports were less than 40 per cent as great as those of the United States in 1913, and its exports were only a little more than a third as great.

The imports through the port of New York alone are one and a half times as great as those of the entire Russian Empire, while New York exports commodities of a hundred million dollars greater value than the whole of Russia sends into the channels of international trade.

# Young Russia   The Land of Unlimited Possibilities          85

### STATUE OF PETER THE GREAT: PETROGRAD

This is one of the most notable of all the world's great equestrian statues. The great stone base is an enormous boulder as large as a medium-sized house, and was brought from the Gulf of Finland, eight miles away, on a specially constructed railway, and over a specially built bridge across the Neva. The horse is treading on an adder and its tail sweeps the serpent's body. This assists a 10,000-pound counterweight in maintaining the equipoise of the horse (see page 23).

Anyone who has seen Russia's leading seaport, Petrograd, marvels that Russia has been able to export as much as she has done. The city is built on a marsh as far north as the southern tip of Greenland. Its waters freeze hard before Thanksgiving and do not melt before the end of April and all its commerce must pass in or out by a canal from Kronstadt, 23 feet deep and 17½ miles long.

### A TREASURE HOUSE

Russia is immensely rich in undeveloped mineral resources. Billions of tons of coal await the pick and shovel, vast deposits of iron ore lie ready for the coming of the railroad and blast furnace, and rich oil deposits already have placed Russia second only to the United States in the production of petroleum. The Empire,

TWO RUSSIAN SOLDIERS IN THE FUR MARKET: PETROGRAD

### NATIVES OF BAKU, RUSSIA

Baku is one of the chief depots for trade between Russia and Persia. Some of the largest oil refineries in the Empire are located here, the wells of the Apsheron Peninsula being like those of the Gulf of Mexico region.

**RUSSIAN RESERVES PROCEEDING TO JOIN THE COLORS AT PETROGRAD**

The almost inexhaustible supply of men Russia has available for war may be shown by a few figures. Approximately two-ninths of the population of the United States is made up of men between the ages of 18 and 44, inclusive. Applying that ratio to Russia—and Russia has a larger proportional male population than we have—the result is 38,000,000 men of military age. Nor is that all. The annual crop of boys reaching the age of 18 years approximates 1,400,000.

in fact, is bountifully supplied with almost every kind of mineral deposit in the category, from asbestos to zinc.

The Ural Mountains region seems to be one of Nature's principal treasuries of mineral wealth. Here nearly all of the world's platinum is mined, the annual output ranging around 200,000 ounces. The Ural iron-ore deposits appear to be almost limitless, and already they are producing four-fifths of all the pig-iron used in Russia. There is a profusion of precious stones; the diamond, sapphire, emerald, tourmaline, topaz, and amethyst, as well as garnet, jade, beryl, aquamarine, and chrysoberyl, are found imbedded in the solid sides of the rugged Urals. Most of the porphyry, jasper, and malachite used in the adornment of the important buildings of Petrograd and Moscow, and which give them that inimitable beauty which every tourist notes, came from this great treasure-house.

There are extensive gold deposits in Siberia, its mines producing about $25,000,000 worth of the precious metal annually. Eleven thousand gold-miners are employed in normal times in the mines of western Siberia, and 30,000 in those of eastern Siberia.

The wages in eastern Siberia are 83 cents a day, while those in western Siberia often are as

Young Russia    The Land of Unlimited Possibilities

ALLEGORICAL STATUE, MAN CONQUERING THE BRUTE:
FONTANKA BRIDGE, PETROGRAD, RUSSIA

The visitor to Russia admires the virile statues and monuments in Petrograd and Moscow. Usually these are the work of Russian artists, who are very successful in expressing action and power (see also page 2). For achievements in music, literature, sculpture, and painting during the past century few people excel the Russians. The fame of Tolstoi, Turgeniev, Vereshchagin, and many others is world-wide.

### THE CATHEDRAL OF ST. ISAAC'S AT PETROGRAD

When the bleak north turns luxurious it can devise splendors to rival those of India, as Petrograd's magnificent cathedral well establishes. St. Isaac's, a huge pile in the form of a Greek cross, of granite blocks and bronze entableture without, a bewilderment of richest marbles within, columns of lapislazuli and exquisite jade, panels of malachite, sanctuaries in snowy and colored marbles, profuse with the works of artists, among them the sculptor Vitali, a prodigal marvel of bronze, marble, gold, and silver, is the peerless church of the Tsar's capital. The interior decorations cost more than twenty million dollars (see p. 98).

    Nearly a thousand years had passed since the birth of Christ before the Russian Slavs were converted to Christianity. Already the English, the Franks, and the Germans had been Christians for some centuries, when, in 987, Prince Vladimir sent envoys to study the religions of the various neighboring nations whose representatives had been urging him to embrace their respective faiths. Nestor describes their report in amusing terms. Of the Mussulmans they reported, "There is no gladness among them, only sorrow and a great stench; their religion is not a good one." At Constantinople they said "we no longer knew whether we were in heaven or on earth, nor such beauty, and we know not how to tell of it." Vladimir thereupon received the missionaries from Constantinople, was baptized, and helped to convert his countrymen.

**SCENE AT PETROGRAD IN FRONT OF ST. ISAAC'S CATHDRAL**

Petrograd is built on the site of ancient marshes which were half under water when Peter the Great selected the location for his new city. The imagination cannot comprehend the great labor that was required to bring the many thousands of huge piles to the city site and to drive them into place. The street in front of St. Isaac's lies over one of these marshes, and it is said that the pile foundation of this structure alone cost a million dollars. Boston, New York, and Philadelphia were thriving communities when Peter drove the first stake for his city, which has become a magnificent metropolis, with wide imposing avenues and immense open squares.

low as 10 cents a day. The men in the mines of eastern Siberia work morning, noon, and night, recognizing neither Sunday nor feast day. The government finds that in this way it can prevent the riotous debauchery of the mining camp and can send the miner home for the winter with money for his family.

While Russia produced one-fifth of the world's petroleum in 1910, its oil industry is not in as satisfactory a state as that of the United States. In 1900 the production of the United States amounted to 2,672,000,000 gallons, as compared with 3,030,000,000 for Russia. In 1910 the production of the United States had

### THE HARBOR OF HELSINGFORS, FINLAND

Helsingfors is located several hundred miles farther north than Sitki, Alaska, and yet it is a busy and growing metropolis of 159,000 inhabitants. Its population expanded 25,000 in less than five years ending in 1908. The harbor of Helsingfors is protected by the great fortress of Sveabord, called the Gibralter of the North.

reached 8,801,000,000 gallons, while Russia's output had fallen to 2,850,000,000 gallons.

Across Russia's broad reaches, extending from 18 degrees east of Greenwich to 169 west, there is a great belt of forest containing 900 million acres that is the finest timbered area still intact on the face of the earth. While wood is still almost the universal fuel, no land-owner is allowed to convert his forest lands to other uses, if the clearing of the land has not been provided for in some general enactment, until he has first notified the government of his intention and received its permission.

No forests essential to the water supply may be cut, and cattle are not allowed to graze on reforested areas until the young trees are 15 years old, or have reached a height of 10 feet.

All forest areas considered protective against erosion by water or the shifting of sands are exempt from taxation.

### RUSSIAN INDUSTRIES

Russia ranks third among the countries of Europe in the number of cotton spindles in operation. Out of the 131 million cotton spindles in the world, 54 million are in Great Britain, 28 million in the United States, 10 million in Germany, and eight million in Russia. Besides 137,000 automatic and 2,000 hand looms operated by mules, there were about 40,000 hand looms operated by peasants. The 750 factories employed about 388,000 hands. The Russian manufacturers last year asserted

**THE LUTHERAN CHURCH OF ST. NICHOLAS: HELSINGFORS, FINLAND**

The culture of the capital of Finland is Swedish. The people of Finland are the best educated of any in Russia, illiteracy there being no higher than in Western Europe. Women were admitted to the right of suffrage in Finland in 1906.

LOADING WHEAT FOR EXPORT AT ODESSA, RUSSIA

Founded by Catherine the Great of Russia, in 1792, soon after the extension of the dominion of the Empire to the shores of the Black Sea, Odessa is a comparatively new city, and its aspect is that of a busy modern West Europe metropolis. Its famous boulevard of Nicholayevsky, lined with rows of over-arching trees, is one of the beauty spots of Russia. The city lies near the great rivers, the Dnieper and the Dniester, which make it one of the great grain-handling ports of the world, yet not a ton of its business can reach the high seas without the permission of the Sultan of Turkey, for it has to pass through the Bosphorus and the Dardanelles, which he controls.

that if they could buy they could use $100,000,000 worth of our cotton annually, but that most of it was sold several times before reaching the mill owner, thus making the price to him too high, with no advantage therein to the producer himself. Before the war Russia was producing $300,000,000 worth of cotton goods annually, using raw cotton to a value of $120,000,000, $48,000,000 being the value of the portion coming from the United States. An import duty of nearly six cents a pound is levied on raw cotton entering Russia.

Employees in Russian factories must be given all the holidays of their respective church, whether orthodox or otherwise. A factory employing a thousand hands must maintain at least a ten-bed hospital. Damages for the death of a workman, as a result of an accident occur-

### A VILLAGE IN THE CENTRAL CAUCASUS MOUNTAINS, RUSSIA

Geographically the Caucasus forms a part of the boundary line between southeastern Europe and western Asia. But it is not merely a geographical boundary marked on the map with a red line and having no other existence; it is a huge natural barrier, 700 miles in length and 10,000 feet in average height, across which, in the course of unnumbered centuries, man has not been able to find more than two practicable passes.

ring while in the discharge of his duties, must be paid to the needy members of his family.

Wages in Russia are very low. A common laborer in Petrograd receives about forty cents a day, and a carpenter seventy cents. At Moscow the monthly wages of men in factories are from five to eight dollars, and of women from three to six dollars.

The hours of labor are long—from ten to eleven and a half hours—and yet so anxious are the peasants who work in the factories to learn to read and write that they often go, after the long, hard day's work in the factory, to night schools.

### THE JEWS

More than half of the 13 million Jews in the world live in Russia, where they are officially called "Those who follow the Mosaic Creed." While the rest of the world—Germany, Austria, France, and Spain—were persecuting these people Poland was offering them asylum, and they

**PEOPLE AT CHEGEM, CENTRAL CAUCASUS, RUSSIA**

The Caucasus region is the ethnological museum of the world. Pliny quotes Timosthenes as saying that in ancient Colchis 300 different languages were spoken, and adds that the Romans required the services of over a hundred interpreters to conduct affairs. Strabo mentions 67 different peoples and tongues in his day in the Caucasus region, and wrote of the poisoned arrows, spiked shoes, and troglodyte caves of that territory. See George Kennan's fascinating account of the Caucasus, "An Island in the Sea of History," in the NATIONAL GEOGRAPHIC MAGAZINE, September, 1913.

accepted that haven as a God-given refuge. When Poland was partitioned the bulk of its Jewish population went with Russia's share, and that is how Russia came to get its Jewish problem.

The Jews in Russia have had a very hard time of it for generations. An alien race prospering where the native race goes hungry naturally arouses bitterness, and that is what has caused the Russian government to adopt such strenuous restrictive measures against the Jews. Instances of this repression is written into every chapter of Russian law. There is a double tax on Kosher meat, first on the animal and then on the meat itself; there is a tax on religious candles used by the Jews; the head of the family must pay a tax for the privilege of wearing a skull-cap during prayers; not more than 10 per cent of the students of a university may be Jews. The laws forbid the Jews to settle outside of the urban districts of the 114 towns embraced in what is known as the "Pale of Jewish Settlement." Many do settle outside and live in peace until a storm arises on the political horizon, when they absent themselves until it blows

PEOPLE OF BERINGI, CENTRAL CAUCASUS, RUSSIA

It was up the ancient Phasis, draining a southern valley from the Caucasus, that Jason sailed to gain the Golden Fleece, and in Colchis that he plowed his acres in the field of Mars. It was to the Caucasus that Hercules went to wrest the magic belt from Queen Hippolyte that made the Amazons of Daghestan such redoubtable foes. It was over the northern steppes of these mountains that poor Io, beset by Juno's gadfly, wandered in aimless torture.

over. No office is open to a Jew unless he renounces his religion, which only a fraction of 1 per cent of them ever do.

Russia feels that domestic policy requires these restrictions of the Jews. Without them, and unfettered, the wide-awake Jew would be too much for the lethargic Slav, say such authorities as Samuel Wilkinson.

### A PROHIBITION NATION

The abolition of the sale of intoxicants in Russia represents the greatest prohibition victory of the age. With one dash of the pen one-sixth of the earth's surface and one-tenth of its population went "dry." Heretofore vodka-drinking has been the curse of the Russian masses. Being a government monopoly, the officials of the government encouraged the sale of vodka, and the constantly and rapidly growing revenues from that source showed that they did so with success.

Then the war came on. Realizing that a drunken soldier can never be a good soldier, the Tsar prohibited the sale of vodka temporarily and inhibited his troops from using intoxicants in any form.

Over night hundreds of thousands of government dram shops were closed. The response of the Russian people to this order was one of the surprises of Russian history. Everywhere it was received with acclaim, and there were such

#### A PASS IN THE CAUCASUS MOUNTAINS: RUSSIA

The entire length of the Caucasus, measured along the crest of the central ridge, does not much exceed 700 miles, but for that distance it is literally one unbroken wall of rock, never falling below 8,000 feet and rising in places to heights of 16,000 and 18,000 feet, crowned with glaciers and eternal snow.

widespread and universal evidence of the approval of the government's stand in the matter that it soon became evident to the Tsar that what he had intended as a temporary measure could be made permanent.

The result was that Tsar Nicholas has answered a petition of the Russian Christian Temperance Society, presented by the Grand Duke Constantine, by saying:

"I have decided to prohibit forever the government sale of alcohol."

And so prohibition, the Russians hope, has come to a great Empire that probably more than any other in history has suffered from the evils of intemperance.

### RUSSIAN SHRINES AND CHURCHES

Whoever has been so fortunate as to visit Russia can never forget her wonderful church music and numberless shrines. Three of her imposing cathedrals are pictured in this book—pages 49, 81, and 90—and are doubly interesting because they show what modern art can do. Being built on the lines of the Greek rather than the Roman cross, the interior is wider in proportion to the length than is permitted by the design of western cathedrals, and this added width gives the Russian edifice an impressiveness all its own.

### KIRGHIZ WOMEN AND GIRLS: WESTERN SIBERIA

Russia has a wonderful list of races and peoples within its confines—Slavs, Lithuanians, Iranians, Latins, Teutons, Finns, Turks, Tatars, Mongolians, Georgians, and Circassians—and the most of these races are divided again into from two to a dozen different peoples. Four million Tatars, a million and a half of Bashkirs, nearly five million Turkomans, and a million and a half of Georgians indicate something of the vastness of the Babel of modern Russia. The Slavs, of course, vastly predominate, with approximately two-thirds of the population. The Kirghiz are closely related by ties of blood to the Mongolians, and by ties of speech to the Tatars. They have preserved to this day the features of the former and the tongue of the latter. Those who live in the upland region trace their descent back to a legendery king, Kirghiz, sprung from Oghuz-Khan, ninth in descent from Japheth.

We had seen the famous cathedrals of Europe—the noted structures of France, Germany, England, Italy, and Sancta Sophia, in Constantinople—but were utterly unprepared for the splendor anti brilliancy of St. Isaac's at Petrograd! Pillars 30 feet high of lapis lazuli and malachite, altar rails of solid silver, containing half a ton of this precious metal; icons of pearls, studded with huge diamonds, sapphires, emeralds, and rubies!

### TEMPORARY FARM OF A SIBERIAN FARMER

Many thousands of peasants annually journey from European Russia to Siberia, pioneers such as were those hardy Americans who pressed westward across the Alleghanies a century ago and laid the foundations of the wonderful progress of the Mississippi Valley. The government does everything within its power to encourage them, even buying agricultural machinery and reselling it to them on the installment plan.

### IMMIGRANTS FROM RUSSIA ARRIVING IN SIBERIA

Such people as these undoubtedly will prove to be the progenitors of a race that will compare with our own sturdy farmers of the Northwest. A group of Russian peasants emigrated to Siberia with nothing but the clothes on their backs, a little flour, some hometanned leather, and a few tools for carpentry and blacksmithing. The first day they made two sets of ovens out of brick they prepared from a clay-bed near by, and the men burned charcoal while the women made bread. Within two days after their arrival they had six blacksmith's forges going, and inside of ten days they had built themselves rude houses, made wagons, manufactured spades by the dozen, and reshod their horses, all the iron used being forged on the ground; yet none of them could read or write.

And then added to the appeal to the eye is the appeal to the other senses. The ear is charmed by the beauty of the voices of priests and deacons rising in waves of sound to the responses of the service. No instrumental music distracts the attention from the human voice. And so beautiful is the singing that one does not miss the organ. The singing, incense, the lights of many candles, the gorgeously-robed priests and deacons, passing in and out against the golden background, all make an irresistible appeal to the emotions.

The icons are the symbols of the saints and of God. In every Russian home, in every room in your hotel, in the railway waiting-rooms, everywhere there is an icon. It is not proper to sit with one's back to it. It consecrates the home, and is a reminder to the Russian that "God is in the midst"—not locked up in the church, but always present. The representations of Christ, of angels, and of saints are given in relief or mosaic or are painted.

The pictures accompanying this passage, showing peasant and gentleman at devotion—pages 6, 12, 20, 21, 47, and 56—are actual snapshots. None of them were posed or planned; similar scenes may be seen every moment everywhere in Russia. His religion is very real to the Russian, and his God is really omnipresent to him; he sees His Spirit everywhere, and everywhere acknowledges it with the sign of the cross and the words, "Oh Lord! have mercy," or "Glory be to Thee, Oh Lord."

## RUSSIA AND THE UNITED STATES

In our own country Russia has always stood by us against the world. Even back in the days of George III, when that monarch appealed to Catherine II of Russia to lend him soldiers to help put down the rebellion in America, writing her an autograph letter in that behalf, the Russian empress disdained to answer him in her own hand, but through her prime minister said she could not help but reflect on the consequences which would result for their dignity if they went jointly to calm a small rebellion which was not supported by any foreign power. This reply, as well as the way of sending it, angered George very much, and he said that she might at least have replied without using expressions that could not be pleasing to ears more civilized than those of the Russians.

Again, in 1812 Russia evidenced her friendship for the United States. She proposed to mediate and thus to settle the differences between the United States and Great Britain. President Madison accepted the proposal and nominated Albert Gallatin and James A. Bayard to act in conjunction with John Quincy Adams in the negotiations; but the Senate refused to confirm the nomination of Gallatin on the ground that he still held the Secretaryship of the Treasury, and so the peace proposals fell to the ground and the war was fought out. When Alexander II freed the serfs of Russia the United States Congress passed a complimentary resolution and sent it to St. Petersburg by a special envoy. The incident pleased the Tsar greatly, and a little later he returned the compliment with interest. His minister to Washington, intimate friend of Slidell and Benjamin, did all that he could to prevent secession, but after Fort Sumter was fired on Russia came out for the Union.

In 1863 the English Government had become seriously stirred as a result of the war. What happened to our trade when the present war broke out was small in comparison with what our civil war did for Great Britain. Hundreds of thousands of people in the textile mills were thrown out of work because American cotton was not to be had. Intervention was openly discussed. Gladstone had hailed Jefferson Davis as a man who had made a nation, and even Lord Palmerston was inclined to lend ear to suggestions of forcing a peace in some way. Finally the English government sounded France with reference to a sort of enforced mediation. About this time, however, a Russian fleet made an ostentatious visit to the port of New York and the social functions that accompanied the visit put England on notice as to where Russia stood, and England's interest in stopping the war suddenly ceased.

## FINAL IMPRESSIONS

There are conditions in Russia which a visitor from the land of free schools, free speech, and a free press finds it difficult to understand; the deplorable rarity of good schools, making it a sore trial for a poor man to get his son educated; the arrival of his American newspaper, with often half a page stamped out by the censor in ink so black that it is impossible to decipher a single letter; the timidity, nay fear, of some people of being overheard when talking frankly on political subjects; the enormous power concentrated in the hands of one individual. But other writers have written with needless emphasis and length on these unpleasant themes, and it is not necessary to discuss them here.

The purpose of this book has been to set forth the immensity of the great land empire, in size four times larger than the Roman Empire at its greatest; to visualize some of the common sights and customs among a kindly and noble race by the use of many unposed photographs; to show the tremendous vitality and fecundity of the Russian people, more than half of whom lived in bondage in the lifetime of thousands of our readers; and to explain the youth of Russia as a nation, showing how she threw off her foreign yoke in the same quarter century that Jamestown was founded and the Pilgrim Fathers landed at Plymouth, and how she is in some respects younger even than the United States, for our ancestors brought from England and Holland institutions wrought through centuries of hard testing, and a blood and brain trained for self-government through many, many generations.

But with all the ignorance and poverty of the masses in Russia in the past, the leaven of national intelligence has begun to work. The government is following the example of our own country in trying to take the gospel of good farming to the peasantry, showing the peasant how to make wholesome butter and more per cow; showing him how to grow more bushels of wheat and rye and oats to the acre; bringing him better blood for his horses and his cattle and his sheep. The progress of the times has also brought the moving picture and the telephone and the railroad into a thousand remote communities, and has set to work forces that inevitably will spell the doom of illiteracy and ignorance and make Russia in fact the land of unlimited possibilities.

# FURTHER READING

Brian Moynahan, *The Russian Century: A Photographic History of Russia's 100-Years* (1994). Nicholas V. Riasanovsky, *A History of Russia* (1984). Robert Service, *A History of Twentieth-Century Russia* (1998). Archie Brown *et al.*, *The Cambridge Encyclopedia of Russia and the Soviet Union* (1982).

# INDEX

Agriculture, 33–35
    future of, 35–37
    stock-raising, 39
Alcohol, prohibition of, 63, 97–98
Alexander II, 32, 81, 102
Assumption, Cathedral of the, 14
Azov, 25

Baku, 87
Bells, 2, 16, 17, 18
Birth rate, 4, 78
Black Forest, 34

Carriage, of aristocrat, 64
Carts, 2, 62, 82
Caucasus, 96, 97, 98
Chegem, 96
Children
    girl, in Moscow, 74
    of priests, 42
    schoolboys in Moscow, 27, 69
    treatment of, 26
    wealthy, 73
    *See also* Education
Churches
    architecture of, 98
    the Assumption, Cathedral of, 14
    experience of, 102
    in Moscow, 6
    Our Savior, Cathedral of, 20, 48, 49, 80
    the Resurrection, Cathedral of, 81
    St. Basil's Cathedral, 31, 75
    St. Issac's, Cathedral of, 90, 99
Circassians, 68
Clothing
    of bride and groom, 58
    of Caucasus, 96, 97
    of Circassians, 68
    of coachmen, 43
    for funeral, 33
    of gypsies, 72
    of Kirghiz, 99
    of laborers, 34, 70

    medals, 5
    of museum attendants, 41
    of nuns, 37, 52
    peasant, 60
    of peasant farmers, 76, 77
    Russian blouse, 69
    shawl, 74
    uniforms, 5, 23, 86
Constitutional Democrats, 45, 50
Convent Novo-Devitschy, 35
Cossacks, 65
Council of State, 82
Court of Arbitration, 82
Crops, 34–35

Drosky, 43
Duma, 45, 50, 82

Education
    and illiteracy, 40, 51, 60–61, 64
    school enrollment, 42, 45
    universities, 50–51

Foreign trade, 83–85
Forestry, 92
Funeral, 33

Geography, 1, 3, 4
Germany, foreign trade with, 83–84
Golden Horde. *See* Tartars
Goudonov, Boris, 15, 16
Grand National Assembly, 23
Great War, 83
Greek Orthodox Church, 8
Gypsies, 72

Hague peace conferences, 71, 82
History
    Alexander II, 32
    famine, 19
    of Moscow, 7–8, 10, 13
    Peter the Great, 23–27
    Polish rule, 22

Romanovs, ascension of, 23
Slavs, 4, 6–7
Tartar rule, 10, 19
Horses and horsemanship, 64

Iberian Chapel, 47
Icons, 24, 102
    peddler, 36
    shops for, 40
Industry, 92, 94–95
Ivan III, 7–8, 9
Ivan the Terrible, 10, 13

Jews
    cloth market, 39
    laws regarding, 96–97
    Polish origins of, 95–96
    taxes on, 96

Kirghiz, 99
Kremlin
    Assumption, Cathedral of the, 14
    battlements of, 9
    Beautiful Redeemer Gate, 11, 12, 13
    bell tower, 15
    central importance of, 69
    history of, 7
    Our Savior, Cathedral of, 20, 48, 49, 80
    St. Basil's Cathedral, 31, 75
    Terem, 83
    Tsar's cannon, 28
    view of, 8

Laborers
    characteristics of, 34
    clothing of, 70
    hours of, 95
    rights and benefits of, 94–95
    wages of, 88, 91, 95
Literacy
    prevalence of illiteracy, 40, 51, 60–61, 64
    street signs, 39
    and women, 40

Medals, 5
Medals of service, 3
Military
    available men for, 88
    Cossacks, 65
    soldiers, 86
Mineral resources, 85, 88, 91–92
Minin, 22
Monastery of Miracles, 19
Moscow
    bazaar, 41
    coachman in, 43
    Convent Novo-Devitschy, 35
    history of, 7–8
    icons shops, 40
    Monastery of Miracles, 19
    Napoleon in, 27–28
    street scene, 38
    in winter, view of, 50
    *See also* Kremlin

Napoleon, 10
    defeat of, 29–32
    in Moscow, 27–28
Nepeia, 10
Nicholas II, 70–71, 82, 97–98
    wealth of, 64–65, 69–70
Nizhni-Novgorod
    bell cart, 2
    university, 2
    Volga River, view of, 51, 52
Novgorod, destruction of, 10
Nuns, 37, 52

Odessa, 94
Oil industry, 91–92
Our Savior, Cathedral of, 20, 48, 49, 80

Peasants
    farmers, 76, 77, 78, 82
    in Nizhni–Novgorod, 57, 59, 60, 61
Peter the Great, 23–25
    death of, 27, 66
    reforms of, 26

# INDEX

statue of, 85
visit to London, 25–26
Petrograd
    Resurrection, Church of the, 81
    St. Issac's, Cathedral of, 90
    view of, 67
    in winter, 67, 85
Pojarski, 22
Population
    agrarian, 33
    available for military service, 88
    diversity of, 1, 41, 99
    growth of, 4, 78
Priests
    black and white, 22
    clothing of, 52
    families of, 42
    as teachers, 45
Prohibition, 63, 97–98

Redeemer Gate, 11, 12, 13
Reforms
    of Alexander II, 32
    of Nicholas II, 82
    of Peter the Great, 26
Religion
    conversion of Vladimir, 90
    Greek Orthodox Church, 8
    *See also* Churches; Nuns; Priests; Shrines
Resurrection, Church of the, 81
Romanov, Michael, 23
Russia
    agriculture, 33–37, 39
    diversity of, 1, 41, 99
    education, 40, 42, 45
    foreign trade, 83–85
    history of, 4, 6–8, 10, 13, 19, 22–27
    industry, 92–95
    land-locked geography of, 4
    mineral resources of, 85, 88, 91–92
    Napoleon in, 27–32
    population of, 4, 33, 78
    size of, 1, 3
    ukase and agrarian reform in, 32
    and United States, relations of, 102–103
    women, position of, 45, 50–51, 60–61, 64

St. Basil's Cathedral, 31, 75
St. Issac's, Cathedral of, 90, 99
Shrines
    Iberian Chapel, 47
    in Moscow, 6, 38, 46
    in Nizhni-Novgorod, 56
Siberia
    farms in, 100
    immigrants, 101
    mines in, 91
    wages in, 88, 91
    women in, 99
Slavs, history of, 4, 6
Sophia Paleolgus, 7–8, 20
Statues
    custom of voting on, 2
    at Fontanka Bridge, 89
    of Peter the Great, 85

Tartars
    merchant, clothing of, 54
    rule of, 7–8, 10, 19
Terem, 83
Transportation
    boats, on river, 55
    carriage of aristocrat, 64
    carts, 62, 82
    drosky, 43
    electric cars, 38
    horses, 64
    tram cars, on ice, 67
Tsar. *See* Alexander II; Ivan III; Ivan the Terrible; Nicholas II; Peter the Great
Turks, Azov campaign against, 25

Ukase, 32
Uniforms, 5, 23
United States, relations with Russia, 102–103
Ural Mountains, 88

## INDEX

Vodka. *See* Alcohol
Volga River, 51, 55

Wages
    in factories, 95
    in Siberia, 88, 91
Wilkinson, Samuel, 97
Women
    and children, visiting icons, 24
    farmers, 76, 77
    literacy among, 40
    nuns, 37, 52
    peasants, 60, 61
    position of, 45, 50
    in Siberia, 99
    wages of, 95
Work hours, 95

Yermak, 10

# CONTRIBUTORS

General Editor FRED L. ISRAEL is an award-winning historian. He received the Scribe's Award from the American Bar Association for his work on the Chelsea House series *The Justices of the United States Supreme Court*. A specialist in American history, he was general editor for Chelsea's *1897 Sears Roebuck Catalog*. Dr. Israel has also worked in association with Arthur M. Schlesinger, jr. on many projects, including *The History of the U.S. Presidential Elections* and *The History of U.S. Political Parties*. He is senior consulting editor on the Chelsea House series *Looking into the Past: People, Places, and Customs*, which examines past traditions, customs, and cultures of various nations.

Senior Consulting Editor ARTHUR M. SCHLESINGER, JR. is the pre-eminent American historian of our time. He won the Pulitzer Prize for his book *The Age of Jackson* (1945), and again for *A Thousand Days* (1965). This chronicle of the Kennedy Administration also won a National Book Award. He has written many other books, including a multi-volume series, *The Age of Roosevelt*. Professor Schlesinger is the Albert Schweitzer Professor of the Humanities at the City University of New York, and has been involved in several other Chelsea House projects, including the *American Statesmen* series of biographies on the most prominent figures of early American history.

5/2001

947.08
S Schlesinger, Arthur Jr.
The Russian People
in 1914

**Portage Public Library**